ESCAPE THE LIE. PROTECT YOUR CLIENTS. RECLAIM YOUR CAREER.

KEEP THE CASH

The $26 BILLION
Scam

Hiding in Your Mortgage Career

UNLOCKED

A LOAN OFFICER'S GUIDE
TO BREAKING FREE FROM
THE INDUSTRY'S BIGGEST SCAM

MICHAEL DENDY

"I HAVE 12 KIDS...I HAVE TO CLOSE LOANS!"

MI 1632279 | Edge Home Finance Corporation supports Equal Housing Opportunity.
NMLS ID# 891464 (www.nmlsconsumeraccess.org). Interest rates and products are subject to change without notice and may or may not be available at the time of loan commitment or lock-in. Borrowers must qualify at closing for all benefits. This is not an offer to lend and each borrower must qualify on their own merit to purchase a home.

LEGAL NOTICE

DEDICATION

To my beautiful bride, Melissa "Bo"! Who has walked beside me since we were just a couple of high school kids with big dreams. You've been my anchor, my encourager, my home and you are "my person". Through every high and low, especially the valleys we never saw coming, your faith and fierce love never wavered. This wouldn't exist without you.

To our twelve amazing children and our growing tribe of grandbabies. You are my legacy and my greatest joy. And to the One who's carried us through it all, Jesus, this is for Your glory. Everything good in my life has come from Your hand.

Family, faith, and a whole lotta grit—that's what built this.

Dendy's 10-Step Transition Process
Your Roadmap from being robbed to Keeping The Cash

Step 1: **Run Your Numbers**
Use the Compensation Calculator to compare your actual retail net income against the 2.75% model and calculate your annual gap.

Step 2: **Have the Kitchen Table Conversation**
Share the numbers with your spouse, partner, or wise counsel and get full family support before taking any action.

Step 3: **Consult an Employment Attorney (if necessary)**
Review your non-compete, non-solicitation, and all employment agreements to know exactly what is enforceable.

Step 4: **Connect With Me To Talk To Edge Home Finance**
Have a transparent conversation with leadership, see the technology, and review real commission statements.

Step 5: **Talk to Loan Officers Who Have Made the Move**
Hear the real transition experience from loan officers who came from your type of company.

Step 6: **Secure Your Personal Relationships**
Ensure personal contact information for referral partners and past clients is stored on your personal devices.

Step 7: **Build Your Financial Bridge**
Set aside 60 to 90 days of living expenses so you transition from a position of strength, not anxiety.

Step 8: **Submit Your Paperwork and Transfer Your License**
Complete the Edge onboarding package and initiate your license transfer, which takes 7 to 14 business days.

Step 9: **Give Notice with Grace**
Resign professionally with a brief meeting and a short letter, then prepare for the predictable phone call.

Step 10: **Launch Your Business and Keep the Cash**
Go live, reconnect with your Realtors, close your first loans, and see 2.75% on a transparent commission statement.

About Michael Dendy

Michael and Melissa grew up in Marietta, Georgia. As high school sweethearts, they have been married for 33 years. Michael and his wife have 12 kids, 2 daughters-in-law, 1 son-in-law, 2 grand-babies, a dog named Kylo and a turtle named Tot.

After closing hundreds of transactions and seeing the need for a consumer advocate in the real estate and mortgage industry, Michael decided to write this book to expose the industry insider secrets for all consumers.

Michael and Melissa have worked hard to provide key insights that will help their kids navigate through some of life's toughest challenges and biggest decisions. He now compiled a tool that is the same information that he would share with his own kids and wants to help homebuyers realize the dream of homeownership.

"I HAVE 12 KIDS...I CLOSE LOANS!"

Follow on social media, check out michaeldendy.com or email at michael@dendyteam.com

You can reach Michael Dendy by calling him directly at 615-499-6335.

A Note To The Reader

When I published *Homebuying Made Easy for Veterans* in 2019, I was inspired by the stories of service members who had sacrificed so much and deserved a smooth, rewarding path to homeownership. Writing that book taught me the importance of simplifying what can feel like an overwhelming process. It also reminded me that no matter where you start, the journey to owning a home is one of the most transformative experiences in life.

Now, I have also written Homebuying Secrets for Veterans, Homebuying Secrets for First-Time Homebuyers and Homebuying Secrets for the Self-Employed and UNLOCKED: The $847 Billion Theft Hiding In Your Mortgage. All dedicated to the same concept of making the homebuying process easier and educating homebuyers.

As I write this book for exposing the industry and making sure loan officers understand the importance of transparency, My passion for helping other loan officers that are in the same situation that I was in hasn't changed. It's grown! I've seen firsthand how daunting the process can be, from budgeting to being scared, to the "I don't know what I don't know and how the mortgage companies intentionally hides the secrets. That's why I wanted to create a resource that not only demystifies the compensation but also inspires confidence and allows loan officers to become "THE CEO LOAN OFFICER".

Of course, I bring a unique perspective to the table. If you've heard my slogan, you know: *"I HAVE 12 KIDS… I HAVE TO CLOSE LOANS!"* That's more than just a catchphrase; it's a testament to my drive and dedication. With a full house of personalities, dreams, and future homeowners under one roof, I've learned the value of hard work, resilience, and keeping things simple.

This book is not just a guide. This book is a conversation. It is a conversation with you, the loan officer. It's the advice I would give my own kids if they were navigating a company change and how I would help them not get "ripped off" by the mortgage industry.

Let's get started!
Michael Dendy
615-499-6335

TABLE OF CONTENTS

THIS PAGE IS INTENTIONALLY LEFT BLANK.

I'VE ALWAYS WANTED TO BE ABLE TO SAY THAT.

I'VE ALWAYS WANTED TO LET CONSUMERS KNOW THAT THIS IS SUCH A WASTE OF PAPER, JUST LIKE THE PAGE THAT IS LEFT BLANK ON YOUR BANK STATEMENT.

IT'S STUPID!

INTRODUCTION

INTRODUCTION
The Long Road to Keeping What You Earn

Let me tell you something about the mortgage industry that nobody is going to tell you at your next company rally or regional sales meeting. Nobody is going to say it from the stage at your annual conference or your "Top Producers Club" trip to the islands. Your branch manager sure is not going to bring it up during your next one-on-one. And the corporate recruiters who sweet-talked you into your current seat? They would rather chew glass than admit what I am about to lay out for you in this book. You are being robbed.

Not in the way that makes the evening news. Nobody is breaking into your house or skimming your checking account. (Well...at least not directly) This is the kind of robbery that happens in plain sight, with your full cooperation, while the people doing it shake your hand, pat you on the back, and tell you what a great job you are doing. It is a systematic, industry-wide extraction of wealth from the people who actually do the work of originating mortgage loans, and it has been happening for so long that most loan officers do not even realize it is going on. I know, because I was one of them. For years.

I got into the mortgage business in Ann Arbor, Michigan. Started at a retail mortgage bank like most people do, full of energy and grateful for the opportunity. They gave me an office, a desk, a phone, access to their systems, and a comp plan that paid me 100 basis points on every loan I closed. One percent. That sounded reasonable to me at the time, because I did not know any better and nobody was handing out comparison charts at orientation.

What they did not put in the welcome packet was the part about my loan officer assistant. See, they gave me an assistant to help with my files, which felt like a real perk when I was getting started. What they failed to mention up front was that any bonus I wanted to pay that assistant came out of my commission. Not the company's pocket. Mine. So that 100 basis points I thought I was making? After I took care of the person helping me do the job they hired me to do, it was less. And the company sat back and collected the rest of the revenue on every single deal I brought in the door without breaking a sweat.

But I worked hard. I am a grinder by nature, always have been. I built relationships, I earned referrals, I showed up early and stayed late. Eventually I worked my way up to branch manager, which came with a raise (sort of) to 125 basis points. That felt like a real accomplishment at the time. I remember calling my wife Bo and telling her about the promotion like I had just won the lottery.

A quarter of one percent raise. That was the big prize for managing an entire branch.

Looking back on it now, I want to reach through time and shake myself. Not because I was stupid, but because the system is designed so well that 125 basis points genuinely felt like I had arrived. The company had set the floor so low that a tiny bump felt like a windfall.

That is how the psychology of retail mortgage compensation works, and it works beautifully for the people on the other side of the equation.

Life had other plans for us, as it tends to do. Bo and I moved our family down to Franklin, Tennessee, and that move changed everything about how I saw this business. Not right away, mind you. The first thing I did was walk into another trap, but at least it was a different kind of trap, and sometimes you have to try on a few bad shoes before you figure out what actually fits.

I took a position with the company I worked for that was now operating a joint venture inside a real estate office. The pitch sounded fantastic. I would be embedded right there with the agents, first in line for every buyer who walked through the door. Built-in referral pipeline. No cold calling. No chasing leads. Just sit at your desk and let the deals come to you.

The comp plan had two tiers. Anything that came from the real estate office, any deal that was captured because I was sitting in their building and one of their agents handed me a client, paid me 80 basis points. Anything I sourced on my own, through my personal network and my own marketing, paid 125 basis points. Same as what I made as a branch manager back in Michigan.

Now, think about that for a second. I had moved my family over 700 miles, uprooted twelve kids, left everything familiar behind, and my best-case scenario was making the same thing I made before. And the deals that were supposed to be the whole reason for taking the job, the ones from the real estate office, actually paid me less than what I was making in Ann Arbor. I was going backwards on the very deals that were sold to me as the golden opportunity.

The joint venture model has a way of looking generous from the outside while being stingy on the inside. The real estate company gets a mortgage operation under their roof without spending a dime on overhead. The mortgage broker gets a captive referral source. And the loan officer? The loan officer gets the privilege of doing all the work for less money, while two companies split the upside above his head. A joint venture like this is built to make money for 2 people, the real estate broker and the mortgage company.

I lasted a while because the deal flow was decent and Franklin is a beautiful place to raise a family. But the more I learned about where the money was actually going on each transaction, the more that 80 basis points started to eat at me. I was not building wealth. I was building someone else's business model, and I was doing it in a nicer zip code than before. The real estate broker decided he found some grass that was greener and ended the joint venture just 5 months into me moving my family across the country.

That is when I made the call that felt like progress. I had a buddy who was working at an independent mortgage broker shop, and every time we talked, he would drop little hints about how much better the economics were on his side of the fence. Not in a pushy way. Just matter-of-factly, the way you might mention to a friend that the restaurant they keep going to charges twice as much as the place down the street for the same steak.

I called him on a Tuesday afternoon and said I was ready to talk. Two weeks later, I was hired on a split. Sixty percent to me, forty percent to the company, on an average commission of 2.25 percent. I remember sitting at my kitchen table with a calculator running the numbers over and over because I could not believe what I was seeing.

On a $350,000 loan at 2.25 percent total commission, the gross revenue was $7,875. My sixty percent cut was $4,725. Compare that to my retail days at 100 basis points, where the same loan would have paid me $3,500 and the company would have kept everything else, including the lender premiums I never even saw. I was making thirty-five percent more per loan without doing a single thing differently. Same borrowers. Same paperwork. Same late nights chasing conditions. Just a different business model sitting underneath me.

That was a real eye-opener. For the first time in my mortgage career, I could see the actual revenue a loan generated before it got divided up. I could see what the lenders were paying, what the total compensation was, and what my share looked like as a percentage of the whole picture. In retail, all of that was hidden behind a curtain. At the broker shop, the curtain was pulled back, and the view from the other side was both thrilling and infuriating. Thrilling because the money was better. Infuriating because I realized how much I had left on the table for all those years in retail.

But here is the thing about progress. Sometimes what looks like the finish line is really just another bend in the road.

The broker shop I was working with decided to get into the correspondent lending business. If you are not familiar with that term, here is the short version. A correspondent lender uses what is called a warehouse line of credit to fund loans in their own name before selling them to a larger lender. On paper, it sounds like a natural evolution for a growing mortgage company. More control, more revenue, more opportunity.

In practice, what it meant for me as a loan officer was that the company now controlled the rate sheets again.

Let that sink in for a moment, because this is one of the most important distinctions in the entire mortgage industry and almost nobody talks about it. When a broker shop operates as a true broker, the loan officer can see the wholesale rate sheets from hundreds of lenders. You know exactly what each lender is charging, what the premiums are, and where the money goes. Transparency is baked into the model because the loan officer is the one shopping the rates.

But when that same broker shop picks up a correspondent warehouse line, everything changes. Suddenly the company is funding loans with their own money, which means they control the pricing. They can mark up the rates, bury premiums, and create their own internal rate sheets that look nothing like what the wholesale lenders are actually offering. The loan officer goes right back to being in the dark about true loan economics, just like retail. The company calls it growth. I call it a bait and switch.

I watched it happen in real time. The rate sheets started looking different. The margins got wider. My split was still sixty-forty, but sixty percent of a smaller number is still a smaller paycheck. The transparency I had fallen in love with when I first went broker started to evaporate, replaced by the same kind of corporate-controlled pricing I thought I had left behind in Michigan. It was retail mortgage banking wearing a broker costume, and I was not about to play that game again.

That is when I found Edge Home Finance, and that is when I made what I firmly believe will be the last NMLS move of my career.

Edge operates as what I call a true broker. Not a broker with a correspondent warehouse line bolted on the side. Not a broker-in-name-only that controls pricing behind the scenes. A true, transparent mortgage brokerage where the loan officer can see every wholesale rate sheet, every lender premium, every basis point of revenue on every single transaction. Nothing is hidden. Nothing is marked up in the shadows. Nothing disappears between the lender and your commission statement. And that word, transparency, is the whole ballgame.

When you operate in a truly transparent broker model, you can see exactly how much revenue your loans generate. You can see what the lenders are paying. You can see where every dollar goes. And when you can see all of that clearly, you can make informed decisions about your business, your pricing, your borrowers, and your career. You stop being a cog in someone else's machine and start being the "CEO Loan Officer" of your own operation.

The model at Edge is cheaper for the loan officer because there is no bloated management pyramid extracting value at seven layers above your head. It is faster because you are not waiting on corporate committees and regional approvals to get deals done. And it is easier because the technology works for you instead of against you, and the compliance infrastructure exists to support your business rather than to justify its own budget by finding reasons to fine you.

Cheaper. Faster. Easier. And completely transparent.

That is not a sales pitch. That is just math. And by the time you finish this book, you will be able to do that math yourself.

I did not write this book because I am angry, although I will admit there were plenty of angry moments along the way. I wrote it because I spent years moving through every version of the mortgage compensation model, from retail employee to joint-venture originator to broker on a split to broker under a correspondent warehouse line, and I learned something at every single stop. What I learned, more than anything else, is that the mortgage industry has perfected the art of taking money from the people who earn it and redistributing it to the people who manage them. It is legal, it is common, and it is costing the average retail loan officer somewhere between $100,000 and $150,000 a year in lost income.

That is not a typo. And that is not a guess. The math is in Chapter Two, and I invite you to check it against your own numbers.

This book lays out twelve specific ways that retail mortgage banks and even some broker shops extract wealth from loan officers. Some of these methods are obvious once you see them. Others are so deeply embedded in the business model that most loan officers have never thought to question them. All twelve of them are costing you real money, real wealth, and real freedom.

After the twelve ways, I am going to give you seven questions. These are the questions your manager does not want you to ask, because the honest answers to these questions expose the entire extraction model for what it is. You do not need to be confrontational. You do not need to be angry. You just need to ask the questions calmly, write down the answers, and then decide for yourself whether the deal you are getting is the deal you deserve.

And then I am going to show you the alternative. Not in vague terms or abstract promises, but with real numbers and a real comparison tool at keepthecash.com where you can plug in your own production and see exactly what your career looks like on the other side of transparency.

I have twelve children. Twelve. That is not a typo either. When you have that many mouths to feed, that many futures to fund, and that many little faces looking at you across the dinner table, you do not have the luxury of leaving money on the table because the system told you to be grateful for what you are getting. Every dollar matters. Every basis point matters. Every year you spend in a model that takes sixty percent of what you generate is a year of wealth that your family will never get back.

My wife Bo has been with me through every single one of these moves. From Ann Arbor to Franklin, from retail to joint venture to broker to correspondent to true broker. She believed in me when I said it was time to go, every single time. And every single time, the numbers proved her faith was well placed. Not because I got luckier with each move, but because each move brought me closer to a model where I could actually keep what I earned.

That is all this book is really about. Keeping what you earn. Keeping The Cash that your talent, your relationships, your late nights, and your hard work generate. Not giving it away to a management pyramid that does not close loans, does not talk to borrowers, and does not lose sleep over whether your deal is going to make it to the closing table on time. You earned it. You should keep it.

The vault has been locked your entire career. This book is the combination.

Let us open it together.

Part 1:
THE HEIST

Chapter 1:
I'VE BEEN ROBBED

The Day I Discovered I'd Been Robbed

"Too many people forget to mind their own business. They spend their lives minding someone else's business and making that person rich."

Robert Kiyosaki, Rich Dad Poor Dad

The coffee was cold by the time I finally looked up from my spreadsheet.

It was almost midnight on a Thursday, and I was sitting at my kitchen table in Franklin, Tennessee, surrounded by old settlement statements, commission reports, and a calculator that had seen better days. Bo had gone to bed a couple hours earlier, shaking her head at me the way she does when I get obsessed with something. She kissed the top of my head and told me I was spiraling. She was right. But I could not stop, because the numbers on my screen were telling me a story that nobody in my entire mortgage career had ever bothered to tell me, and once I started reading it, I could not put it down.

Three weeks earlier, I had been sitting at a closing table with a veteran named Tony and his wife. Beautiful couple. Three kids. This was their first home purchase, and you could feel the emotion in that room the way you feel a summer thunderstorm building over the hills. I had spent three months getting this deal done. VA guidelines, tight debt-to-income ratio, a seller who almost walked twice, and a family that needed me to hold their hand through every hiccup along the way. The kind of loan that makes you remember why you got into this business in the first place.

We were signing documents, and I was watching them tear up as they got their keys, and everything felt right with the world. Then the closing attorney slid the settlement statement across the table. Tony, being sharp the way most military folks are, started reading through every single line. He asked about the origination charge. He asked about the discount points. He asked about the processing fee. I walked him through all of it, because that is what a good loan officer does.

Then he looked up at me with this expression that I will never forget, kind of half confused and half amused, and he said something that broke my brain.

"Michael, all these fees add up to about thirteen thousand dollars. You told me your commission is around one percent. That's about three thousand five hundred on our loan. So where's the other ten thousand going? And what about the rate markup? I did some research. I know what rates are supposed to be."

I stood there with my mouth open. Not because the question was rude. It was not. It was the most reasonable question in the world. I stood there with my mouth open because I did not have a good answer. I had a corporate answer. I had the talking points they trained me to give. But I did not have the real answer, because I had never actually done the math myself.

And that bothered me more than anything Tony could have said.

That is how I ended up at my kitchen table at midnight with cold coffee and a pile of loan files. I had pulled every single closed loan from the past year. Forty-seven of them. And I was doing arithmetic that apparently nobody else in the mortgage industry wanted me to do.

I will walk you through one deal so you can see what I saw.

Loan number one was a purchase at $350,000. The rate was 4.5 percent. My commission came out to about $3,500 at my comp plan. The borrower paid $2,800 in discount points. Total origination charges on the settlement statement added up to around $13,000. That all seemed fine on the surface, the way a lake looks fine from the shore until you wade in and realize the bottom drops off six inches from the edge.

I pulled the actual rate sheet from that day. The lender's par rate, which is the rate where the lender makes money but does not pay or charge points, was 3.625 percent. My borrower got 4.5 percent. That 0.875 percent difference meant my borrower was paying about $1,602 per year in extra interest, and over a thirty-year mortgage, that adds up to more than $48,000 in additional interest payments. But here is the part they never taught me at any training session or company rally. That rate markup generated what the industry calls secondary pricing. The investor pays a bonus to the company or broker for delivering a loan at a higher rate than par. On that particular loan, the true rate that the loan was sold on the secondary market was roughly 450 basis points, which translated to about $15,750. I did not see this was happening at all. My rate sheet was stacked against me.

So let me add that up for you the way I added it up for myself at midnight with shaking hands and cold coffee. The total revenue that loan generated was approximately $15,750 when you combined my commission, the borrower-paid fees, and the lender basis points. My cut was $3,500. The company kept the other $12,250. I did one hundred percent of the work on that deal. I found the borrower. I took the application. I gathered the documents. I fought with underwriting over conditions at ten o'clock at night. I held Tony's wife's hand when she cried because she thought the deal was falling apart. I coordinated the closing. I showed up with a smile. And for all of that, I kept twenty-two cents of every dollar that loan generated. Twenty-two percent. The company kept seventy-eight percent.

And they did not find Tony. They did not sit at his kitchen table explaining VA loan benefits. They did not call him back on a Saturday to calm his nerves. They did not do any of the work that made that loan happen. But they took the majority of the money.

I went through all forty-seven loans that night and the next three nights after that. The numbers varied from deal to deal, but the pattern was the same every single time. On average, the total revenue per loan was somewhere between $12,000 and $16,000 when you factored in everything, including the investor buying the loan from the company and what was collected but never shown to me. My average take-home was between $3,200 and $4,100 per loan, depending on the deal structure. That meant I was keeping somewhere between twenty-five and thirty-five percent of the revenue I generated, and the company was keeping the rest.

Forty-seven loans in a year at an average extraction of roughly $8,000 to $10,000 per loan that I never saw. That is somewhere between $376,000 and $470,000 in a single year that I generated with my labor, my relationships, and my expertise, and the company pocketed without breaking a sweat.

I sat back in my chair and stared at the ceiling. The house was dead quiet. Everyone was asleep. And I felt something that I can only describe as a combination of nausea and fury, the kind of feeling you get when you realize you have been conned, not by a stranger on the street, but by the very people you trusted with your career.

I was not angry because the company was making money. Companies should make money. I was angry because the split was so dramatically one-sided, and I had never even known it. I was angry because nobody had ever shown me the full picture. I was angry because I had been a top producer, a loyal employee, a branch manager who brought in revenue and trained junior loan officers, and the entire time, the company was taking three to four dollars for every one dollar they paid me, and calling it competitive compensation.

Here is what I want you to understand about that night at my kitchen table, because it is the reason I wrote this book.

The hard part was not the math. The math is simple. Any loan officer with a calculator and a rate sheet can figure out what I figured out in a few late nights. The hard part was accepting what the math meant. It meant that for years, I had been building someone else's wealth while being told I was building my own. It meant that every pat on the back, every award at the company, every "great job, Michael" from my regional VP was delivered while they were quietly collecting three times what they paid me on every deal I closed. It meant I had bought into a narrative that was specifically designed to keep me in my place, producing at a high level and never questioning the economics underneath me.

Robert Kiyosaki wrote about this exact phenomenon in Rich Dad Poor Dad, and when I read his words years later, I felt like he had been sitting at my kitchen table that night. He talked about how people spend their entire lives minding someone else's business, making someone else rich, without ever stopping to ask whether the arrangement makes sense for them. That is exactly what I had been doing. I was minding the company's business. I was making the company rich. And I was so busy doing it, so focused on closing the next loan and hitting the next production goal, that I never stopped to mind my own business and ask the obvious question: where does all the money actually go?

Once I asked that question, everything changed. Not overnight, and not without a lot of uncomfortable conversations and a fair amount of fear. But the question itself was the crack in the dam. Once the water starts coming through, there is no patching it.

I want to be real with you about something before we go any further in this book. I am not the sharpest tool in the shed. I am not a financial genius. I am not some Ivy League MBA who figured out a market inefficiency using advanced algorithms. I am a former pastor from Georgia that moved to Michigan who ended up in the mortgage business because life took me there, and I have twelve kids to feed, which means I do not have the luxury of leaving money on the table because the system told me to be grateful. If I can figure this out, you can figure this out.

The only difference between the loan officer who sees the extraction and the loan officer who does not is whether somebody shows them where to look. That is what this book does. I am going to show you where to look. I am going to walk you through the twelve specific ways retail mortgage banks and even some broker shops extract wealth from loan officers. I am going to give you seven questions to ask your manager or owner that will either confirm your company is one of the rare good ones, or expose the extraction for exactly what it is. And then I am going to show you what the alternative looks like, with real numbers and a real comparison tool, so you can decide for yourself whether the deal you are getting is the deal you deserve. But before any of that, I need you to do one thing.

I need you to pull your last few commission statements or paystubs. Pull the settlement statements from your recent closings. If you can get your hands on the actual rate sheet from the day those loans locked, pull that too. And then sit down at your kitchen table, or your desk, or wherever you do your best thinking, and do the math. Figure out what the total revenue was on each deal. Not just your commission, but the whole picture. The borrower-paid fees. The secondary market basis points. The rate spread. Everything. Then calculate what percentage of that total you actually took home.

If that number is somewhere between twenty-five and forty percent, you are in the same boat I was in. And this book is going to show you exactly how to get out of it.

If you cannot get the information you need to do that math, if the rate sheets are hidden, if "secondary market" is not disclosed, if your manager gets uncomfortable when you ask about total loan economics, then that tells you something all by itself. Companies that have nothing to hide do not hide things. And the fact that you cannot see the full revenue picture on your own production is the first and most important sign that the system is not designed in your favor.

The coffee was cold. The house was quiet. My spreadsheet was staring back at me with numbers that could not be argued with and could not be unseen. I closed my laptop and sat in the dark for a long time.

When Bo came downstairs the next morning, I was already up. Already showered. Already had a fresh pot of coffee going. She took one look at my face and knew something had shifted.

"You figured it out," she said. It was not a question.

"Yeah," I said.

"I figured it out."

"How bad is it?"

"Bad enough that we need to talk about what happens next."

I poured her a cup of coffee, she sat down across from me, and said the five words that changed the trajectory of our family's financial future.

"Okay. Tell me everything."

That is exactly what I am about to do for you.

In the next chapter, we follow the money. Where does $26 Billion in extracted loan officer compensation actually go, and how did the industry build a machine so effective that an entire generation of originators never thought to question it?

Chapter 2:
FOLLOW THE MONEY

CHAPTER 2

Follow the Money

"You cannot make profits and transfer the risks to others, as bankers and large corporations do. Forcing skin in the game corrects this asymmetry better than thousands of laws and regulations."

Nassim Nicholas Taleb, Skin in the Game

You are probably wondering where the number $26 billion comes from. I wondered the same thing when I first started running the calculations, because it seemed impossible. It seemed like the kind of number someone makes up to sell books or get clicks on a headline. But the math is straightforward, and I am going to walk you through it right now so you can check it yourself. Here is how you get to $26 billion.

According to industry data, there are approximately 230,000 retail mortgage loan officers working in the United States at any given time. That number fluctuates with market conditions, but I'm going to use half of that number. 115,000 is a reasonable baseline and it is the number I will use throughout this book. The average retail loan officer produces somewhere between $10 million and $20 million in annual loan volume, depending on the market and their experience level. For our purposes, I will use $15 million, which is conservative and sits right in the middle of what most mid-career loan officers produce.

On that $15 million in volume, the total revenue generated per loan officer, when you factor in origination fees, lender premiums, rate spread revenue, and ancillary income, conservative averages somewhere between $350,000 and $600,000 per year. Again, I will use the conservative end. Let us say $375,000 in total annual revenue generated per loan officer.

Now here is the number that changes everything. The average retail loan officer takes home between thirty-five and forty percent of the total revenue they generate. Some get less. Very few get more. The rest, that sixty to sixty-five percent, goes to the company. It goes to management overrides, corporate overhead, technology fees, compliance departments, marketing budgets, executive compensation, shareholder returns, and a dozen other line items that you never see on your commission statement.

At the conservative estimate of $375,000 in total revenue and a forty percent take-home rate, the average retail loan officer earns about $150,000 per year. The company keeps $225,000. Multiply that $225,000 extraction across 115,000 loan officers, and you get almost $26 billion per year. Over twenty years, which represents a reasonable career window in the mortgage industry, that cumulative extraction exceeds $520 billion. Adjust for the years when the market was hotter and volumes were higher, and the number climbs well past $700 billion.

That is not a typo. That is not hyperbole. That is arithmetic.

WHERE YOUR LOAN REVENUE ACTUALLY GOES

Average retail loan officer on a typical $375,000 loan

($375,000 in total annual revenue generated)

	Company Keeps (60%)	You Keep (40%)
Revenue Category	Retail LO	True Broker
Your Annual Income	$150,000	$300,000+
Company / Overhead Takes	$225,000	$40,000
% of Revenue You Keep	35-40%	85-90%
Your 20-Year Earnings	$3,000,000	$6,000,000+
20-Year Wealth Gap		$3,000,000+

Take a long look at that chart. The column on the left is where you are right now. The column on the right is where you could be, doing the exact same work, closing the exact same loans, serving the exact same borrowers. The only difference is who keeps the revenue.

Now let me show you how the industry got here, because this was not an accident. The modern retail mortgage model did not evolve naturally. It was engineered, and understanding how it was built is the first step to understanding why it works so well at keeping loan officers in the dark.

Before the 2008 financial crisis, the mortgage industry looked very different. Most loan officers were independent. You hung your license with a mortgage broker, or you were the broker yourself. You had relationships with multiple lenders. You shopped rates for your clients. You got paid based on what you produced, and the typical split was seventy-thirty or eighty-twenty in the loan officer's favor. Retail mortgage departments existed at the big banks, sure, but they were mostly for existing bank customers. The broker channel was dominant, and loan officers kept the majority of the revenue they generated. Then the housing market collapsed, and everything changed.

When the dust settled from the crash, thousands of small broker shops were gone. The big banks survived because they had deep balance sheets and government bailouts. The Dodd-Frank Act and subsequent regulations dramatically increased the cost of compliance, which hit small brokers harder than large institutions. The narrative shifted overnight. Suddenly brokers were the villains who caused the crisis. The big banks, who had been packaging toxic mortgage-backed securities and selling them to pension funds, somehow came out of the wreckage looking like the responsible adults in the room.

That narrative was a lie, but it was an effective one. And it paved the way for the largest consolidation of mortgage talent in the history of the industry. Between 2008 and 2015, the number of independent mortgage brokers dropped by more than sixty percent. Those loan officers had to go somewhere, and the retail banks were waiting with open arms and carefully designed compensation plans that paid just enough to feel reasonable while extracting the majority of the value.

The retail banks did not just absorb the talent. They built an entire infrastructure designed to keep that talent from ever leaving again. Non-compete agreements. Proprietary technology systems that locked in your data. Management hierarchies that created psychological loyalty. Brand prestige that made loan officers feel important for wearing the logo. Benefits packages that created dependency. And comp plans that were complex enough to obscure the extraction but simple enough that nobody questioned them.

It was brilliant, really. In the span of about seven years, the retail banks went from holding a minority of the loan officer market to dominating it. And the loan officers who joined them, many of whom had been independent brokers making seventy to eighty percent of their revenue, accepted thirty-five to forty percent and called it a good deal because the alternative had been made to look dangerous.

There is a word for this kind of arrangement, and it is not a comfortable one. But it is accurate, and I am not in the business of making you comfortable. I am in the business of telling you the truth.

The word is **sharecropping.**

In the old sharecropping system, a farmer worked land that belonged to someone else. The landowner provided the property, maybe some tools, maybe some seed. The farmer did all of the actual work. Planting. Tending. Harvesting. Sweating through the summer heat and praying for rain. And when the crop came in, the landowner took the majority of the harvest. The farmer kept whatever was left, which was never quite enough to get ahead, never quite enough to buy his own land, and never quite enough to break free from the arrangement.

The system was designed that way on purpose. If the farmer could save enough to buy his own plot, he would leave. And if he left, the landowner lost his labor. So the economics were carefully calibrated to keep the farmer productive but dependent. Earning enough to survive, but never enough to be free. Now look at the retail mortgage model.

THE SHARECROPPER PARALLEL

Side-by-side comparison of two extraction models separated by 150 years

	1870s Sharecropper	Modern Retail LO
Who does the work?	The farmer	The loan officer
Who provides the platform?	The landowner (land, tools, seed)	The bank (license, LOS, brand)
Who keeps the majority?	The landowner (60-70%)	The bank (60-65%)
Can the worker leave?	Technically yes, practically no (debt traps)	Technically yes, practically no (non-competes, fear)
Who owns the output?	The landowner owns the crop	The bank owns the database
Can the worker build equity?	No	No
What keeps them there?	Debt, fear, no alternatives	Non-competes, fear, narrative

I know that comparison makes some people uncomfortable. Good. It should. Because the economic mechanics are identical even if the historical context is different. A system that takes sixty percent of what you produce, prevents you from building equity, controls the tools of your trade, claims ownership of your output, and uses a combination of financial pressure and psychological manipulation to keep you from leaving is an extraction system. Whether the person doing the extracting wears overalls or a corner office suit does not change the math.

Let me show you something that will make this even more concrete. One of the most effective tools retail banks use to suppress loan officer compensation is the management pyramid. This is the chain of people who get paid a percentage of your production without ever touching a loan file, talking to a borrower, or showing up at a closing table.

When I ask retail loan officers how many people get paid when they close a deal, most of them say two or three. The real answer is usually seven to twelve. Here is what the typical management extraction chain looks like for a loan officer producing $15 million per year at a mid-size retail mortgage bank.

THE MANAGEMENT PYRAMID OF EXTRACTION

Who gets paid from YOUR production at $18 million annual volume

Management Layer	Override / Allocation	Annual Cost to You
You (the loan officer)	35-40% of revenue	$150,000
Branch Manager	8-15 bps override	$14,400 - $27,000
Area / District Manager	3-8 bps override	$5,400 - $14,400
Regional VP	2-5 bps override	$3,600 - $9,000
Divisional SVP	1-3 bps override	$1,800 - $5,400
National Production Head	Allocated salary/bonus	$2,500 - $5,000
C-Suite Executives	Allocated comp	$3,000 - $8,000
Corporate Overhead	Allocated cost	$35,000 - $55,000
TOTAL EXTRACTED		$65,700 - $123,800

Every single person on that list above your name gets paid whether your deal closes smoothly or nearly falls apart at the eleventh hour. They get paid whether you worked weekends or not. They get paid whether the borrower called you crying at ten o'clock on a Sunday night or not. Their compensation is a function of your labor, and most of them could not pick you out of a lineup.

The branch manager, to be fair, usually knows you exist. The branch manager probably recruited you, probably trained you, and probably provides some genuine value in terms of support and leadership. I am not here to vilify every person in the management chain. But from the area manager up through the C-suite, the value proposition gets thinner with every layer while the extraction stays constant. The regional VP who has never set foot in your branch still collects an override on every loan you close. The divisional SVP who could not tell you the difference between an FHA 203b and a VA IRRRL still gets a taste. And the corporate overhead allocation that funds the home office in Charlotte or Detroit or wherever the mothership sits? That is coming straight out of your production whether you have ever visited the building or not.

This is what suppression looks like. It is not a manager standing over your shoulder telling you to work harder for less money. It is a system of layers, each one siphoning off a percentage of your revenue before it reaches your paycheck, and each one positioned so far above you that you never see the extraction happening. You see your commission statement. You see your take-home pay. But you never see the full revenue picture, because the full picture would make you furious, and furious loan officers start asking questions, and questions are the one thing the management pyramid cannot survive.

THE CAREER COST OF STAYING IN RETAIL

Cumulative wealth gap between retail and true broker over a 20-year career

Career Year	Retail Cumulative	True Broker Cumulative	Wealth Gap
Year 1	$150,000	$300,000	$150,000
Year 3	$450,000	$900,000	$450,000
Year 5	$750,000	$1,500,000	$750,000
Year 10	$1,500,000	$3,000,000	$1,500,000
Year 15	$2,250,000	$4,500,000	$2,250,000
Year 20	$3,000,000	$6,000,000	$3,000,000

That chart does not include investment returns, compounding, or the equity value that an independent broker builds in their own business over time. Those factors would make the gap even wider. This is a straight-line comparison using conservative numbers, and the twenty-year difference is three million dollars.

Three million dollars. That is the cost of staying in a system that was designed to keep you productive but never wealthy. That is the price tag on loyalty to an institution that would replace you in two weeks if you dropped dead tomorrow. That is the retirement you will not have, the college fund you will not build, the generational wealth you will not pass down to your children because someone in a corner office decided that your labor was worth forty cents on the dollar and you believed them.

Nassim Taleb wrote about exactly this kind of asymmetry in Skin in the Game. He argued that you cannot build a fair system when one party takes the profits while transferring the risks to someone else. That is precisely what the retail mortgage model does. The loan officer bears all the risk. You are the one whose phone rings at midnight. You are the one whose income drops to zero if rates spike and the market freezes. You are the one whose reputation is on the line with every borrower and every Realtor. And yet the company takes sixty percent of the revenue from every deal you close, whether the market is booming or busting. They have structured the arrangement so that you carry the risk and they collect the reward.

That is not a partnership. That is not competitive compensation. That is extraction dressed up in a branded polo shirt.

I want to address something before we move on, because I know some of you are thinking it. You are thinking that the company provides value. That they give you leads, and technology, and compliance support, and a brand name, and benefits, and all the infrastructure you need to do your job. And that is true. They do provide those things. I am not suggesting they provide nothing.

What I am suggesting is that those things do not cost what they are charging you for them. The technology that costs you $250 a month in deductions could be purchased independently for $100 a month. The compliance support that supposedly justifies a huge chunk of your lost revenue could be outsourced for a fraction of the cost. The brand name, which they will tell you is priceless, is worth exactly zero to the borrower who chose you because their Realtor referred you, not because they saw a logo on a billboard. And the leads? We will get into the lead scam in detail later, but I can tell you right now that the company is buying internet leads for eight to fifteen dollars each and reselling them to you for ten times that amount.

The value the company provides is real. The price they charge for it is not. And that gap between real value and inflated price is where the extraction lives. That gap is the mechanism that turns a sixty-forty revenue split into something that looks almost reasonable when you are standing inside the system, but looks like highway robbery when you step outside and compare.

In the chapters ahead, I am going to walk you through twelve specific extraction methods, one by one, with real numbers and real examples. I am going to show you the comp plan illusion, the hidden management overrides, the technology markups, the compliance fees, the marketing scams, and the non-compete traps that all work together to keep you earning forty percent of what you are worth.

But I wanted you to see the big picture first. I wanted you to see the $26 billion number and understand where it comes from. I wanted you to see the sharecropper parallel and feel the weight of it. I wanted you to see the management pyramid and count the layers of people who get paid from your sweat. And I wanted you to see the twenty-year career chart and understand that this is not an abstract problem. This is your retirement. This is your children's future. This is real money that belongs to you and is being taken from you, legally and systematically, every single day that you remain in a model designed to extract your value while calling it opportunity.

The system is not broken. It is working exactly the way it was designed to work. It just was not designed for you.

Next, we get specific. Chapter 3 opens the twelve extraction methods with the two biggest ones: the comp plan illusion and the basis point shell game. Pull your last commission statement. You are going to need it.

Part 2:

THE VAULT

Chapter 3:
THE COMP PLAN ILLUSION

CHAPTER 3
The Comp Plan Illusion

"Everything has a price, but not all prices appear on labels."

Morgan Housel, The Psychology of Money

Let me tell you about the day I finally understood comp plans. I was sitting in a training session at my retail bank, the kind that is technically voluntary but where your absence gets noticed, and our regional compensation director was explaining the new comp structure. She had a PowerPoint with forty-three slides. Lots of charts with arrows pointing up. She used the word "competitive" eleven times in the first ten minutes. I know because I started counting.

The new plan looked great on paper. Base commission increased from 85 basis points to 100 basis points. New bonus tier at ten million in production. Accelerators for hitting monthly goals. Enhanced benefits package. Everyone in the room was nodding along like we had just been handed the keys to the kingdom. The branch manager was smiling. The regional VP who flew in for the meeting was practically glowing. One of the newer loan officers raised his hand and said, "This is amazing. Thank you for fighting for us."

And I sat there in the back of the room with my stomach sinking, because I had just spent the previous three weeks doing the math from Chapter 1, and I knew something that nobody else in that room knew. The new comp plan was worse than the old one.

Not in the obvious ways. The basis points were higher. The bonus tiers were more generous. The accelerators were new. On a surface-level comparison, the new plan was objectively better than what we had before. But what nobody in that room was thinking about, what the forty-three-slide PowerPoint was specifically designed to prevent you from thinking about, was what happened to the rate sheets on the same day the new comp plan rolled out.

Because on the exact same day that our commission went from 85 to 100 basis points, the company quietly adjusted the internal rate sheets. The rates we offered borrowers went up by roughly 12.5 to 25 basis points across the board. Not enough for a loan officer to notice immediately, because rate sheets fluctuate daily with the market. But enough to claw back every penny of the comp plan increase and then some. The company gave us 15 basis points with one hand and took 25 basis points with the other, and then threw a pizza party to celebrate our raise.

That is **Way Number One**. Rate spread theft. And it is the single largest extraction mechanism in the retail mortgage model.

Here is how rate spread theft works in plain English, because the industry has gone to great lengths to make this complicated enough that most loan officers never bother to understand it.

Every lender publishes a rate sheet every morning. That rate sheet lists interest rates and corresponding prices. At the par rate, the lender makes its standard margin and neither pays a premium to the originator nor charges the borrower extra points. Below par, the borrower pays discount points to buy the rate down. Above par, the lender may give a credit to the borrower or just keep it. That premium is called the yield spread premium, or the service release premium, or the lender-paid compensation, depending on which decade you started in this business and what your company calls it.

In a true broker model, the loan officer can see the wholesale rate sheet directly. They know exactly what par is. They know what the points and credits are at each rate tier. They can price a loan transparently, show the borrower exactly what the rate costs, and earn their compensation in a way that is visible to everyone involved.

In the retail model, you never see the wholesale rate sheet. You see the company's internal rate sheet, which has been marked up before it reaches your screen. The company takes the wholesale rates, adds their margin on top, and hands you the adjusted version as if it were the real thing. You price your loans off their sheet, and the difference between the wholesale rate and the retail rate is revenue that the company collects and you never see.

Let me put real numbers to this.

THE ANATOMY OF RATE SPREAD THEFT

A single $375,000 conventional purchase loan, same day, same borrower

	What You See	What Actually Happens
Rate offered to borrower	4.75%	4.5%
Wholesale par rate that day	You don't know	3.75%
Rate markup (spread)	Hidden from you	0.75%
Lender premium on markup	You never see this	2.25 points = $9,375
Your commission (100 bps)	$3,750	$3,750
Total loan revenue	You think: ~$5,000	Actual: $13,125+
YOUR SHARE OF TOTAL REVENUE	You think: ~75%	Actual: ~30%

Read that last row one more time. You think you are earning 75 to 100 percent of the revenue on your loans because you see your commission relative to the small slice of fees that are visible to you. In reality, you are earning about 30 percent of the total revenue that your loan generated. The company collects the other 70 percent, and the largest piece of that is the rate spread premium that you never see, that is never disclosed to you, and that does not appear anywhere on your commission statement.

Morgan Housel wrote something in The Psychology of Money that hit me like a freight train the first time I read it. He said that everything has a price, but not all prices appear on labels. That is the mortgage industry in one sentence. The price you pay for working in retail is not on any label. It is not in your offer letter. It is not in the comp plan document. It is not on the forty-three-slide PowerPoint. The price is hidden inside the rate sheet, buried in the spread between wholesale and retail, and collected by the company on every single loan you close for as long as you work there.

That brings us to **Way Number Two**, which I call the basis point shell game, and this one is even sneakier than the rate spread theft because it uses your own comp plan against you.

The basis point shell game works like this. The company gives you a comp plan expressed in basis points. One hundred basis points. One hundred and ten basis points. Maybe even one hundred and twenty-five basis points if you are a top producer. That number feels meaningful. It feels like a percentage. It feels like you are earning a real share of the business you bring in. But here is what they do not tell you: that basis point number is calculated against the loan amount, not against the total revenue the loan generates.

On a $375,000 loan at 100 basis points, you earn $3,750. That sounds like one percent. And it is one percent of the loan amount. But the total revenue on that same loan, as we just showed, might be $12,187 or more. Your $3,750 is not one percent of the revenue. It is 30 percent. The company uses basis points instead of revenue percentages because basis points make the comp plan look generous. If they told you that your comp plan was 30 percent of total revenue, you would immediately ask where the other 70 percent was going.

But when they tell you that your comp plan is 100 basis points, you do not ask that question, because 100 sounds like a whole lot of something.

It is a shell game. They put the pea under one cup and then move the cups around fast enough that you lose track. The pea is revenue. The cups are basis points, loan amount, and total compensation. And by the time they are done shuffling, you walk away thinking you found the pea when it was in their pocket the whole time.

Now let me tell you about the sign-on bonus, because this is the golden handcuff that the industry has turned into an art form, and it is one of the most effective tools that retail banks use to recruit loan officers and then lock them into a compensation model that costs them far more than the bonus was ever worth.

Here is how it works. A retail mortgage bank wants to hire you. Maybe they are recruiting you from another retail bank, or maybe they are luring you away from a broker shop. They offer you a sign-on bonus. Seventy-five thousand dollars. A hundred thousand dollars. Sometimes two hundred thousand or more for a top producer. They wire the money into your account before you close your first loan, and it feels like Christmas morning. You call your spouse. You pay off a credit card. You buy a boat. Maybe you put a down payment on a new truck. You feel valued. You feel wanted. You feel like this company really invested in you. And they did invest in you. The same way a farmer invests in a cow.

Because here is what happens next. The sign-on bonus is not a gift. It is a loan, typically structured as a forgivable note that vests over two to three years. If you leave before the vesting period is up, you owe the company some or all of that bonus back. That means you are financially trapped. Even if you figure out the rate spread theft. Even if you see the comp plan illusion. Even if you calculate that you are losing $100,000 or more per year in extraction. You cannot leave without writing a check back to the company that is stealing from you.

But the financial trap is only half the story. The other half is what the company does to the rate sheets to pay for the bonus in the first place.

THE SIGN-ON BONUS TRAP

How a $100,000 sign-on bonus actually costs you $300,000+

The Sign-On Bonus Lifecycle	Real Cost to You
Step 1: Company offers $100,000 sign-on bonus	Feels like $100,000 gain
Step 2: Bonus structured as 3-year forgivable note	You are now financially trapped
Step 3: Company widens rate sheets by 15-25 bps to recoup the bonus from your production	You lose $27,000 - $45,000/yr in hidden rate spread
Step 4: Over 3-year vesting period, total extraction from widened spreads	$81,000 - $135,000 in extra extraction
Step 5: You stay beyond vesting because inertia sets in and you rationalize staying	Extraction continues indefinitely
Step 6: Over 5 years total, widened spreads cost you far more than the bonus was worth	$135,000 - $225,000 in extra extraction
NET RESULT: The $100K bonus actually cost you	$35,000 - $125,000+ net LOSS

Read that chart carefully. The company gave you $100,000 and then took back $135,000 to $225,000 over the vesting period and beyond. You did not get a bonus. You took a loan from your own future earnings at a devastating interest rate, and the company structured the deal so that you would feel grateful while they were doing it.

I have talked to many loan officers who took sign-on bonuses. Every single one of them remembers exactly how much the bonus was. Almost none of them can tell you what happened to their rate sheets after they started. That is not an accident. The sign-on bonus is designed to create an emotional anchor, a number you remember and feel good about, that prevents you from noticing the slow, steady extraction that follows.

And the sign-on bonus does something else that is even more damaging in the long run. It creates a culture of job-hopping that looks like opportunity but is actually a treadmill. Here is the cycle. You take a sign-on bonus at Company A. After two or three years, the bonus has vested and a recruiter from Company B calls with a bigger sign-on bonus. You jump to Company B, feeling like you got a raise. Company B widens their rate sheets to cover your bonus. After another two or three years, Company C calls. You jump again. And again. And again.

Every time you jump, you get a check that feels like progress. But every time you jump, you reset the rate sheet trap. You never build equity. You never build a business. You never build anything that belongs to you. You are a free agent bouncing between extraction systems, collecting signing bonuses while leaving the real money on the table at every stop. The companies love this cycle because each sign-on bonus is recouped within eighteen months through widened rate sheets, and after that, it is pure profit for them while you are already counting down to the next recruiter's call.

The loan officers who break this cycle are the ones who stop chasing bonuses and start chasing transparency. They stop asking how much is the sign-on and start asking what is the total revenue on my loans and what percentage of it am I keeping. That second question is the one the industry does not want you to ask, because the answer makes the sign-on bonus look like the bait on a hook. Which is exactly what it is.

THE COMP PLAN ILLUSION: WHAT 100 BPS REALLY MEANS

Same loan officer, $18 million annual volume, 48 loans per year

	Retail at 100 bps	True Broker
Annual volume	$15,000,000	$15,000,000
Your stated comp rate	100 bps (1.00%)	200-275 bps (2.00-2.75%)
Your gross annual income	$180,000	$360,000 - $495,000
Less: tech/overhead costs	Deducted before you see it	($24,000 - $36,000)
Net annual income	$150,000 - $165,000	$324,000 - $471,000
Total loan revenue generated	$375,000 - $450,000	$375,000 - $450,000
% of revenue you actually keep	33 - 40%	85 - 92%
ANNUAL INCOME DIFFERENCE		$159,000 - $321,000 MORE

That chart is the comp plan illusion stripped naked. On the left side, you see what a retail loan officer earning 100 basis points actually takes home when all the hidden extractions are factored in. On the right side, you see what the same loan officer, closing the same volume on the same loans for the same borrowers, takes home in a true broker model where the rate sheets are transparent and the revenue split is honest.

The difference is not 10 percent. It is not 20 percent. It is 100 to 200 percent more income, depending on your volume and the specific comp structure. And the retail loan officer will never see this comparison unless someone shows it to them, because the entire retail compensation model is designed to prevent this math from being done.

Let me tell you about a conversation I had with a loan officer named David in Charlotte. David had been at a major retail bank for nine years. He was a consistent producer, closing about $22 million a year. His comp plan was 110 basis points, which put him right around $240,000 in annual income. He had taken a $150,000 sign-on bonus when he joined the bank, which had fully vested years ago, and he had turned down three recruiter calls in the past eighteen months because he felt loyal to his team and his manager.

I walked him through the math. The same math I just showed you. We pulled up the wholesale rate sheets from a lender we both had access to and compared them to his bank's internal rate sheet.

The markup was 37.5 basis points on average, which on his $22 million volume translated to roughly $82,500 per year in rate spread revenue that David never saw. We added that to the management overrides, the technology markups, the compliance fees, and all the other extractions we will cover in later chapters. When we were done, David was looking at a total annual extraction of approximately $185,000. He was quiet for a long time. Then he said, "So in nine years, they've taken about $1.7 million from me."

"Give or take," I said.

"And the $150,000 sign-on bonus that made me feel like a king?"

"They made that back in the first year. Everything after that was profit."

David did not sleep that night. I know because he texted me at two in the morning with a photo of his kitchen table covered in commission statements and a message that said, "You were right. Every single number checks out."

David is now a broker. He closed $24 million last year and his take-home was just north of $400,000. That is $200,000 more than he made at the retail bank, doing the same job, for the same borrowers, in the same market. The only thing that changed was who kept the cash.

This is the comp plan illusion. It is the foundation that the entire retail extraction model is built on. If loan officers understood that 100 basis points is not 100 percent of anything meaningful, and that the real revenue on their loans is two to four times what they are being paid, the retail model would collapse overnight. Every comp plan negotiation, every recruiter pitch, every sign-on bonus check is designed to keep you focused on the basis point number and away from the revenue number. Because the basis point number makes you feel compensated. The revenue number makes you feel robbed.

Everything has a price, just like Morgan Housel said. The price of working in retail is not on any label. But it is real, it is enormous, and you are paying it on every single loan you close.

The question is whether you will keep paying it now that you know what it costs.

Next, Chapter 4 exposes the hidden bosses. Seven to twelve people get paid a percentage of your production, and you can only name two of them. We are going to name the rest.

Chapter 4:
THE HIDDEN BOSSES

CHAPTER 4

The Hidden Bosses

"As you travel up the hierarchy, the work gets easier, the pay gets better, and the number of people available to do the work gets smaller."

Seth Godin, Linchpin

I want you to try something for me. Pull out a piece of paper and write down every person who gets paid when you close a mortgage loan. Not the people involved in the transaction, like the appraiser or the title company. I mean the people inside your organization who receive compensation that is directly tied to your production. Go ahead. Write them down. I will wait.

If you are like most retail loan officers I have talked to over the years, your list has two or three names on it. You wrote down yourself. You probably wrote down your branch manager. Maybe you included a processing manager or a production assistant if you have one. And then you stopped, because those are the people you interact with and those are the people you think about when you think about your team. Now let me show you the real list.

On a typical retail mortgage loan, somewhere between seven and twelve people inside the organization receive compensation that is directly or indirectly tied to your production. Some of them get a specific override on every loan you close. Others receive a salary or bonus that is allocated across the total production of the office, the region, or the company, which means a slice of your revenue funds their paycheck even though there is no line item with your name on it. These are your hidden bosses. They eat before you eat. They get paid before you get paid. And most of them have never set foot in your office, returned a phone call from one of your borrowers, or stayed up past midnight chasing conditions for a loan that was supposed to close on Friday.

Seth Godin wrote something in Linchpin that has stuck with me ever since I first read it. He said that as you travel up the hierarchy, the work gets easier, the pay gets better, and the number of people available to do the work gets smaller. That is the retail mortgage management pyramid described in a single sentence. The further someone sits from the borrower, the less work they do on any individual deal, and the more money they make from the collective production of the people below them. The loan officer, who sits at the very bottom of the pyramid, does the most work and keeps the smallest share. The executives at the top do none of the origination work and keep the largest share. The hierarchy exists not to support you, but to feed on you.

Way Number Three: The Management Override Tax

Your branch manager gets an override on every loan that closes in the branch. This is one of the few hidden bosses you probably already know about, because good branch managers are visible. They help you solve problems. They run meetings. They recruit new loan officers. They deal with HR headaches and compliance audits. A good branch manager earns their override, and I am not here to tell you otherwise.

What I am here to tell you is what that override actually costs you and how it gets layered on top of every other extraction you are already paying.

The typical branch manager override ranges from 8 to 15 basis points on every loan that closes in the branch. On a $375,000 loan, that is $300 to $563 going to your branch manager from your deal. If you close 48 loans a year, that is $14,400 to $27,000 per year coming out of your production and going to your manager. Now, if your branch manager is genuinely helping you close more loans than you would close on your own, that might be a fair trade. The problem is that many branch managers in the retail model are not primarily focused on helping you produce. They are focused on recruiting, because every new loan officer they bring into the branch adds to the volume that generates their override. A branch manager running a ten-person team at $18 million per officer is collecting overrides on $180 million in production. At 10 basis points, that is $180,000 per year in overrides before their base salary, before their own production if they still originate, and before any bonus they receive for hitting branch targets.

Your branch manager may be your friend. Your branch manager may be an excellent leader. But your branch manager is also a hidden fee built into every single loan you close, and that fee is the same whether they helped you with the deal or not.

Way Number Four: The Regional VP Extraction

Above your branch manager sits the area manager or district manager, and above them sits the regional vice president. These are the people you see at quarterly meetings and annual conferences.

They give speeches about market share and production goals. They hand out awards and shake hands and take photos for the company newsletter. And every single one of them collects an override or a production-based bonus from your loans.

The area manager typically collects 5 to 10 basis points on all production in their territory. The regional VP collects 2 to 5 basis points on all production in their region. Above the regional VP, there is usually a divisional senior vice president who collects 1 to 3 basis points on all production in their division. And above them sits the national production head, the chief production officer, or whatever title the company has invented to put another layer between you and the revenue you generate.

Let me walk you through what this looks like on a single loan.

THE HIDDEN FEE STACK

Every person and fee embedded in a single $375,000 loan

Who Gets Paid	Override / Fee	Per Loan	Per Year (48 loans)
You (the loan officer)	100 bps	$3,750	$180,000
Branch Manager	15 bps	$563	$27,024
Area / District Manager	10 bps	$375	$18,000
Regional Vice President	3 bps	$113	$5,424
Divisional SVP	2 bps	$75	$3,600
Nat'l Production Head	Allocated	$65	$3,120
C-Suite / Executive Comp	Allocated	$105	$5,040
Rate Spread (from Ch. 3)	100+ bps	$3750+	$180,000+
Processing Fee Markup	$350-$600/loan	$695	$33,360
Corporate Overhead Allocation	Varies	$2000+	$96,000+
TOTAL HIDDEN FEES PER LOAN		**$7,741+**	**$371,568+**

YOUR SHARE vs. TOTAL REVENUE	YOU: 32% / THEM: 68%

That chart includes only the fees that I can reasonably estimate from public data, industry averages, and my own experience at multiple mortgage companies. The actual numbers at your company may be higher or lower, but the structure is the same everywhere. Every single loan you close passes through this gauntlet of extraction before your commission hits your bank account. And notice that the rate spread extraction from Chapter 3 is the single largest line item on the list, dwarfing all the management overrides combined. That is by design. The management overrides are small enough per loan that you would never notice them even if someone showed you the numbers. But when you stack them up across a year of production, the total is staggering.

Now ask yourself a question. How many of those people on the chart helped you close your last loan? How many of them talked to your borrower? How many of them chased a condition letter from underwriting at nine o'clock on a Thursday night? How many of them called the listing agent to keep the deal from falling apart?

The answer, in most cases, is one. Your branch manager. Maybe. Everyone else on that chart is a hidden boss who gets paid from your labor without contributing a single minute of effort to the specific deals that fund their compensation. They are organizational overhead disguised as leadership, and you are the one funding their paychecks.

Way Number Five: Corporate Overhead Bloat

The management overrides are irritating, but at least you can point to specific people and argue about whether they provide value. Corporate overhead is a different beast entirely, because it is a fog of expenses that nobody can fully explain and nobody is willing to justify in detail.

Corporate overhead is the catch-all category that includes the home office building, the corporate support staff, the human resources department, the marketing department, the IT infrastructure team, the accounting department, the legal department, the executive dining room, the corporate travel budget, the annual conference, the holiday party, and every other expense that the company incurs at the corporate level and then allocates across the production base. Every dollar of corporate overhead gets spread across every loan that closes, and the loan officers who produce those loans are the ones who pay for it.

Let me give you a sense of the scale. A mid-size retail mortgage bank with 500 loan officers and a corporate headquarters in a major city might have annual corporate overhead expenses of $25 million to $40 million per year. That includes the building lease, the corporate salaries, the technology infrastructure, the conference budget, and all the other expenses that have nothing to do with closing loans and everything to do with running a large organization. Spread that $25 million to $40 million across 500 loan officers producing an average of 48 loans per year, and you get an overhead allocation of roughly $1,000 to $1,700 per loan. Per loan. On top of the management overrides. On top of the rate spread. On top of every other fee.

And here is the part that really gets under my skin. You are paying for things that you do not use, do not need, and in many cases did not know existed. The corporate holiday party that you did not attend because you live three states away from the home office? You helped fund it. The executive retreat at a resort in Scottsdale where the CEO and his direct reports spent four days talking about strategic vision while sipping cocktails by the pool? Your loan production covered a piece of that. The private office of the chief marketing officer who has never generated a single lead for you personally? You are subsidizing their lease, their salary, and their assistant's salary through the overhead allocation embedded in every loan you close.

I want to make this personal for a moment, because I know how easy it is to read about corporate overhead as an abstract concept and shrug it off as the cost of doing business. So let me tell you about a woman named Rachel who worked at a large retail bank in Texas.

Rachel was a strong producer, closing about $24 million a year. She had been with her company for six years and had never once questioned her comp plan because she made good money and the company treated her well. She drove a nice car. She lived in a nice house. She was a top-ten producer in her region. By any visible measure, Rachel was winning.

Then Rachel's company held its annual producer conference at a five-star resort in Palm Beach. The CEO gave a keynote speech from a stage with a fifty-foot LED screen behind him. There were celebrity speakers. There was a gala dinner with a live orchestra. There was a branded photo booth and gift bags with three hundred dollar headphones inside. Rachel told me later that the production numbers they showed on that LED screen made her stomach turn, because for the first time, she could see the total revenue the company generated from all of its loan officers combined, and the number was enormous. She went back to her room that night and started calculating.

The total revenue figure they had displayed, which was well over a billion dollars, divided by the number of loan officers in the company, gave her a per-officer revenue number that was nearly triple what she thought she was generating. She had always assumed her production was worth what the company paid her. Seeing the aggregate number made her realize that her production was worth far more, because the company was collecting from selling loans on the secondary market, investor rebates, servicing income, and half a dozen other revenue streams that she had never been told about.

"They spent a million dollars on that conference to celebrate how much money they made off of us," she told me. "And we clapped."

Rachel is now a broker. She closed $26 million last year, a modest increase over her retail production, and her take-home was $510,000. That is nearly double what she made at the retail bank. She told me the hardest part was not leaving. The hardest part was admitting that she had been fooled for six years by a company that was very, very good at making her feel valued while taking the majority of what she earned.

THE HIDDEN FEE BREAKDOWN: WHERE YOUR REVENUE GOES

Annual allocation for a loan officer producing $15 million / 40 loans per year

Revenue Category	Per Loan	Annual	% of Total
Your Commission	$3,750	$150,000	36%
Selling on Secondary	$2812+	$112,480+	18%
Management Overrides (all layers)	$1296	$51,840	9%
Corporate Operational Support	$2,000	$80,000	12%
Processing Support	$695	$27,800	5%
Retained Hidden Profit / Other	$1,304+	$52,160+	20%
TOTAL REVENUE PER LO	$11,857+	$474,280+	100%
YOU KEEP	$3,750	$150,000	32%
THEY KEEP	$8,107+	$324,280+	68%

That chart is the complete picture. Every dollar that flows through a retail mortgage loan gets divided among these categories, and the loan officer who originated the deal, who found the borrower, who held the relationship together, who did all the work that made the revenue possible, keeps thirty-two cents on every dollar. The other sixty-eight cents goes to a combination of management layers, corporate overhead, rate extraction, and retained profit that the loan officer never sees and rarely knows exist.

And here is the thing that makes this truly maddening. The company will tell you that they need those sixty-eight cents to provide you with the support, technology, compliance infrastructure, and brand recognition that makes your job possible. They will tell you that you could not close loans without them. They will tell you that the overhead is the cost of doing business in a regulated industry.

And they are partially right. There is a cost to compliance. There is a cost to technology. There is a cost to operational support. But those costs do not add up to sixty-eight percent of total revenue. Not even close. In a true broker model, the total cost of compliance, technology, operations, and overhead runs somewhere between fifteen and twenty-five percent of revenue. That means the company is charging you two to four times what those services actually cost, and pocketing the difference as profit that you never see and never share in.

THE REAL COST OF SUPPORT SERVICES

What the company charges you (hidden) vs. what it actually costs on the open market

Service	Retail (Hidden Cost)	True Broker (Actual Cost)
Loan Origination System (LOS)	$200 - $400/mo deducted	$75 - $150/mo actual cost
CRM / Lead Management	$150 - $300/mo deducted	$50 - $100/mo actual cost
Compliance / Licensing	$300 - $600/mo allocated	$100 - $200/mo actual cost
Operational Support	$2,400 - $2,800/loan deducted	$500 - $800/loan actual cost
Marketing / Branding	$400 - $700/mo allocated	$100 - $300/mo (your own)
E&O / Insurance	$200 - $350/mo allocated	$50 - $100/mo actual cost
TOTAL MONTHLY COST	$3,650 - $5,150+/mo	$875 - $1,650/mo
ANNUAL OVERCHARGE		$86,500 - $98,000/yr

That comparison is not hypothetical. Those are real price ranges from real vendors and real broker shops that I have worked with and verified. The retail bank charges you two to three times the market rate for every single support service because you have no alternative and no visibility into the pricing. You cannot shop for a cheaper LOS because the company mandates the system. You cannot negotiate your compliance allocation because it is set at the corporate level. You cannot opt out of the marketing fee because it is embedded in your overhead. You are a captive customer of your own employer, paying marked-up prices for services that are available on the open market for a fraction of the cost.

And the most painful part of all of this? At a true broker like Edge Home Finance, where the compensation is set at 2.75 percent with complete transparency, you can see every one of these costs clearly. Nothing is hidden. Nothing is marked up in the shadows. You know exactly what you are paying for technology, for compliance, for processing, for everything. And because you can see it, you can control it. You can shop for better rates. You can negotiate. You can make informed decisions about where your money goes. You can even adjust the 2.75% if you want to. YOU ARE YOUR OWN CEO!

Transparency is not just a buzzword. It is the mechanism that prevents extraction. When everything is visible, overcharging becomes impossible. When everything is hidden, overcharging becomes the business model. That is the fundamental difference between the retail model and the true broker model, and it is the difference that costs you between $100,000 and $200,000 per year.

I want to close this chapter with something that a loan officer in Atlanta said to me after I showed him these numbers. His name was James, and he had been at a large retail bank for eleven years. Eleven years. He was well-respected, well-liked, and well-compensated by retail standards. When I walked him through the hidden fee stack and the real cost comparison, he sat quietly for a long time. Then he said something that I think about almost every day.

"I have been paying people I have never met, for work they have never done, with money I did not know I was making, for over a decade. And every year at the company dinner, I stood up and thanked them for the opportunity."

James did not cry. He just looked at the numbers on the page, folded his hands, and went quiet for a while. Then he asked me one question.

"How fast can I move my license?"

The answer, as we will discuss later in this book, is faster than you think. But first, we have seven more extraction methods to expose. And they are every bit as infuriating as the first five.

Next, Chapter 5 rips the cover off the technology trap and the compliance racket. Your LOS, your CRM, your quality control fees, and your legal department are all profit centers disguised as support services. We name the names and show the receipts.

Chapter 5:
THE TECHNOLOGY TRAP
AND THE COMPLIANCE RACKET

CHAPTER 5

The Technology Trap and the Compliance Racket

"Being busy is a form of laziness — lazy thinking and indiscriminate action. Being overwhelmed is often as unproductive as doing nothing, and is far more unpleasant."

Tim Ferriss, The 4-Hour Workweek

If you work in retail mortgage, you are surrounded by technology that you did not choose, did not negotiate, and cannot leave behind. Your loan origination system was selected by someone at the corporate level who has never taken a loan application. Your CRM was purchased in a bulk deal that prioritized the company's reporting needs over your ability to manage client relationships. Your compliance tools were implemented by the legal department to protect the company from lawsuits, not to protect you from losing a deal. And every single one of these systems has a cost that is either deducted directly from your commission statement or buried in the corporate overhead allocation that eats into your production before you see a penny.

Tim Ferriss wrote in The 4-Hour Workweek that being busy is a form of laziness. He was talking about individuals who fill their days with activity instead of outcomes, but the same principle applies to organizations. Retail mortgage banks are very busy charging you for technology. They are very busy building compliance departments. They are very busy creating internal systems and processes and quality control checkpoints. What they are not busy doing is asking whether any of those things are worth what they cost, because the people who pay the cost are the loan officers, and the loan officers do not get a vote.

This chapter covers four extraction methods that share a common thread: they are all systems that the company presents as benefits to you while functioning primarily as profit centers for the company. They are the tools and departments that retail banks point to when they justify their sixty-five percent take of your revenue. And every one of them costs two to four times what it should.

Way Number Six: The LOS Scam

Your loan origination system is the backbone of your daily workflow. It is where you take applications, run credit, submit loans to underwriting, track conditions, and manage the pipeline from first call to closing table. You spend more time inside your LOS than any other piece of software, and you cannot do your job without it. Which is exactly why it is such an effective extraction tool.

66

The typical retail mortgage bank selects a loan origination system at the enterprise level and then passes the cost down to the loan officers through commission deductions or overhead allocations. The most common enterprise LOS platforms on the market cost between $40 and $75 per user per month at enterprise scale. Some of the premium platforms cost up to $100 per user per month when you add on all the bells and whistles. Those are real prices that I have verified with multiple technology vendors and broker shop owners who purchase these systems on the open market.

Now here is what your retail bank charges you. The typical LOS deduction on a retail loan officer's commission statement runs between $200 and $400 per month. Some banks charge a flat monthly fee. Others charge a per-loan technology fee of $75 to $150 that shows up on every deal. Either way, the math is simple. The bank pays $50 to $100 per month for your LOS license, charges you $200 to $400 per month, and pockets the difference. On an annual basis, that markup costs you between $1,200 and $3,600 per year. Not a fortune by itself. But stack it on top of every other extraction, and it adds up.

And here is the part that makes it truly insulting. You have no choice in the matter. You cannot shop for a different LOS. You cannot negotiate the price. You cannot switch to a cheaper platform because the company mandates the system, and your data lives inside their infrastructure. You are a captive customer being charged a markup on a tool you are required to use, with no competitive alternative and no pricing transparency. If a landlord did this with utilities, you would call it gouging. When a mortgage bank does it with technology, they call it the cost of doing business.

Way Number Seven: The CRM Con

The customer relationship management system might be even more offensive than the LOS, because at least the LOS is genuinely critical to your workflow. The CRM is a tool that the company gives you, charges you for, and then uses against you.

Let me explain what I mean. Your CRM is where you store your contacts. Your borrowers, your Realtors, your financial planners, your referral partners, your past clients, everyone you have spent years cultivating relationships with. Those contacts are the single most valuable asset you have as a loan officer. They are your book of business. They are your future income. They are the result of thousands of phone calls, hundreds of lunches, years of follow-up emails, and a career's worth of trust-building. And they live inside the company's system, on the company's servers, controlled by the company's technology team.

When you leave a retail mortgage bank, what happens to your CRM data? In most cases, you lose it. The company owns the database. The company owns the contacts. The company owns the notes, the call logs, the relationship history, everything you built over years of work. You walk out the door with whatever you can remember and whatever business cards you can stuff in a box, and the company hands your database to the next loan officer who sits in your chair. And they charged you for the privilege the entire time.

The typical CRM deduction on a retail commission statement is $100 to $300 per month. That is $1,200 to $3,600 per year for a system that stores your data on someone else's server, limits your ability to export your own contacts, and ultimately functions as a retention tool for the company rather than a growth tool for you. The company knows that the longer you use their CRM, the more entangled your business becomes with their infrastructure, and the harder it becomes for you to leave. Every contact you add, every note you write, every task you create is another thread tying you to a system that you are paying for but do not own.

On the open market, a high-quality CRM designed specifically for mortgage professionals costs between $50 and $150 per month. Some of the best options are under $100. And when you own the account, you own the data. You can export it. You can migrate it. You can take it with you when you move. The contacts you built with your labor and your relationships belong to you, not to a corporate server that goes dark the day your employment ends.

THE TECHNOLOGY MARKUP

What you pay in retail vs. what it actually costs on the open market

Technology	Retail Charges You	Actual Market Cost	Annual Markup
Loan Origination System	$200-$400/mo	$50-$100/mo	$1,800-$3,600
CRM Platform	$100-$300/mo	$50-$150/mo	$600-$1,800
Pricing Engine	$75-$200/mo	$30-$75/mo	$540-$1,500
Document Signing / Portal	$50-$150/mo	$20-$50/mo	$360-$1,200
Automated Marketing	$100-$250/mo	$30-$100/mo	$840-$1,800
Per-Loan Tech Fee	$75-$150/loan	$0 (included above)	$3,600-$7,200
TOTAL ANNUAL TECH COST	$9,600-$19,800	$2,160-$5,700	$7,440-$14,100

Take a good look at that chart. The company is charging you $9,600 to $19,800 per year for technology that would cost you $2,160 to $5,700 on the open market. The markup ranges from two to four times the actual cost, and you have no negotiating power because you cannot choose your own tools. In a true broker model, you pick your own LOS, your own CRM, your own pricing engine, and your own marketing platform. You pay market rates for all of them. And because you own the accounts, you own the data, which means your book of business travels with you wherever you go.

Way Number Eight: Quality Control Fees

Every mortgage company has a quality control department. Their job is to audit closed loans for compliance with federal regulations, investor guidelines, and company policies. Quality control is necessary. It protects the company, the investors, and ultimately the borrowers. I am not arguing that QC should not exist. What I am arguing is that QC should not be a profit center.

At most retail mortgage banks, the quality control department is funded through a combination of per-loan fees and overhead allocations that get charged to loan officers. The typical QC fee ranges from $75 to $200 per loan, depending on the company. On 48 loans per year, that is $3,600 to $9,600 annually. And the QC department does not just audit your loans randomly. They audit every loan. Which means you are paying a per-deal fee for a department whose primary function is to protect the company from regulatory risk, not to help you close more business.

Here is the part that makes this extraction particularly frustrating. When the QC department finds an issue with one of your loans, the cost of correcting that issue typically falls on you as well. If a loan needs to be cured, repurchased, or restated because of a documentation error, the financial consequences roll downhill to the loan officer. So you are paying a fee to fund a department that audits your work, and then paying again when that department finds something wrong. The company bears virtually none of the downside risk from QC findings, despite being the entity that profits from the QC fees. That is the definition of a system designed to extract value from the people who do the work while shielding the people who collect the revenue.

In a true broker model, quality control still exists, but the costs are transparent and proportional. The broker pays for QC as part of their operating expenses, and those costs are reflected in the overhead structure that the loan officer can see and evaluate. There are no hidden per-loan QC fees skimming money off the top of every deal. The total cost of compliance is visible, which means it is honest, and honesty is the one thing the retail model cannot afford.

Way Number Nine: The Legal Department That Only Protects the Company

Every retail mortgage bank has a legal department, and that legal department has one job: protect the company. Not you. The company. When you read that sentence, your first reaction might be to shrug and say, of course that is their job. They work for the company. But I want you to think about what that really means in practice, because the implications are more expensive than you realize.

The legal department drafts your employment agreement. The non-compete clause that restricts where you can work after you leave? That was written by the legal department. The non-solicitation agreement that prevents you from contacting your own clients after your employment ends? Legal department. The arbitration clause that forces you to resolve any dispute through a process that historically favors the employer? Legal department. The intellectual property assignment that says anything you create on company time, including marketing materials, client communications, and referral strategies, belongs to the company? Legal department.

Every one of those provisions was designed to protect the company at your expense. The non-compete keeps you from leaving for a competitor, which keeps you trapped in their extraction model. The non-solicitation keeps you from taking your relationships with you, which means the company retains the value of your book of business even after you are gone. The arbitration clause ensures that if you ever figure out the extraction and try to fight it, the fight happens on their turf with their rules. And you are paying for all of it through the overhead allocation that funds the legal department's salaries, benefits, and office space.

You are literally funding the legal team that writes the contracts designed to keep you from building your own wealth. That is not a metaphor. That is a line item.

THE COMPLIANCE AND LEGAL FEE STACK

Annual cost of compliance, QC, and legal overhead allocated to a single loan officer

Compliance / Legal Cost	Retail (Hidden)	True Broker (Visible)
Quality Control Fees	$3,600-$9,600/yr	$1,200-$2,400/yr
Legal Dept Allocation	$2,400-$6,000/yr	$500-$1,200/yr
Regulatory / Licensing Fees	$1,800-$4,200/yr	$800-$1,500/yr
E&O / Fidelity Insurance	$1,200-$3,000/yr	$600-$1,200/yr
Audit / Exam Prep	$600-$1,800/yr	$300-$600/yr
TOTAL COMPLIANCE / LEGAL	$9,600-$24,600/yr	$3,400-$6,900/yr
ANNUAL OVERCHARGE		$6,200-$17,700/yr

Combine the technology markup from the chart above with the compliance and legal fee stack, and you are looking at a total of $13,340 to $33,000 per year in overcharges on support services alone. That is before the rate spread theft, before the management overrides, before the corporate overhead allocation. These are just the fees for the tools and departments that the company tells you are there to help you do your job. And every one of them costs two to three times what it would cost in a transparent broker model.

WAYS 6-9: COMBINED ANNUAL IMPACT

Total extraction from technology, CRM, QC, and legal on a loan officer
producing 48 loans/year

Extraction Method	Per Loan	Annual Low	Annual High
Way 6: LOS Markup	$50-$150	$1,200	$3,600
Way 7: CRM Con + Data Lock-in	$25-$75	$600	$1,800
Way 8: QC Fees	$75-$200	$3,600	$9,600
Way 9: Legal / Compliance Allocation	$125-$300	$6,000	$14,400
Per-Loan Tech Fee (additional)	$75-$150	$3,600	$7,200
TOTAL WAYS 6-9 EXTRACTION	$350-$875	$15,000	$36,600

These four extraction methods are the ones that retail banks love to
defend, because they sound like legitimate business expenses. Technology costs
money. Compliance costs money. Quality control costs money. Legal counsel
costs money. All of that is true. Nobody is disputing that these things have a
cost. What we are disputing is that they cost what you are being charged for
them. The gap between the inflated retail price and the actual market price is
extraction, plain and simple. It is the company using mandatory services as a

markup opportunity, and it is costing you between $15,000 and $36,600 per year on top of every other extraction we have already discussed.

I want to tell you about a loan officer named Todd who worked at a mid-size retail bank in Phoenix. Todd was tech savvy. He actually liked digging into technology and comparing platforms, and one day he got curious about what his LOS would cost if he purchased it independently. So he called the vendor directly and asked for a quote. The enterprise license price was $65 per user per month. His commission statement showed a technology deduction of $325 per month for the same system. When Todd brought this discrepancy to his branch manager, the branch manager told him that the higher cost covered additional integrations and support that the vendor provided at the enterprise level. Todd called the vendor again and asked about enterprise-level support pricing. The vendor told him that enterprise support was included in the $65 per month license.

Todd brought the vendor's quote to his manager, printed out and highlighted. His manager got uncomfortable. The conversation ended with his manager saying, and I am paraphrasing because Todd told me this story with language that is not appropriate for a book, that the company's pricing was not Todd's concern and that he should focus on production.

Todd told me later, "The moment my manager told me the pricing was not my concern, I knew it was exactly my concern."

Todd moved his license three months later. He is producing the same volume, using a better LOS through a direct subscription at market rates, paying for his own CRM that he owns outright, and taking home almost $200,000 more per year. Same loans. Same borrowers. Same technology. Different economics.

There is one more piece to the legal department story that I want to address before we close this chapter, because it is the piece that keeps the most loan officers trapped even after they see the numbers and understand the extraction.

The non-compete agreement.

Most retail mortgage banks require loan officers to sign a non-compete as a condition of employment. These agreements vary in scope and enforceability, but the typical version says that you cannot work for a competing mortgage company within a certain geographic radius for a period of twelve to twenty-four months after leaving. Some include non-solicitation clauses that prevent you from contacting any client you worked with during your time at the company. A few of the more aggressive versions claim ownership of any referral relationships you developed during your employment.

These agreements are the legal department's masterpiece. They do not cost the company much to draft. A template non-compete probably takes an attorney two hours to write and gets reused thousands of times. But the chilling effect on loan officer mobility is worth millions. Every loan officer who stays at a retail bank because they are afraid of their non-compete is a loan officer who continues to generate revenue at a thirty-five to forty percent take-home rate instead of moving to a model where they keep seventy to eighty-five percent. The legal department's $500 template agreement generates millions in retained production every year, and the loan officers who are imprisoned by it are the ones funding the legal department that drafted it.

Here is what I want you to know about non-competes. In many states, they are extremely difficult to enforce against individual loan officers, especially when the loan officer moves to a different business model rather than a direct competitor. The enforceability varies by state, and I am not an attorney, so I strongly encourage you to consult one before making any decisions. But I will tell you this: I have talked to hundreds of loan officers who were terrified of their non-competes, and I have only met a few whose former employer actually pursued legal action after they moved and the company still had no grounds.

Judges don't typically take away a loan officer's ability to provide for their family. The non-compete is not a wall. It is a scarecrow. And it only works as long as you are afraid of it.

Talk to a lawyer. Get real advice about your specific agreement in your specific state. And then decide whether a piece of paper written by a legal department that exists to protect the company, not you, is worth $100,000 to $200,000 per year of your family's future.

Next, Chapter 6 finishes the twelve extraction methods with the three that hit closest to home: the lead program scam, the marketing mirage, and the non-compete trap. These are the tools the company uses to make you feel like you need them. You do not.

Chapter 6:

THE MARKETING MIRAGE
AND THE FINAL INSULT

CHAPTER 6

The Final Insult

"To maintain your independence you must always be needed
and wanted. The more you are relied on, the more freedom
you have. Make people depend on you for their happiness and
prosperity and you have nothing to fear. Never teach them
enough so that they can do without you."

Robert Greene, The 48 Laws of Power

Robert Greene wrote those words as a warning, not as a business plan. He
was describing how powerful people have manipulated others throughout three

thousand years of recorded history, using dependency as a weapon to maintain control. The strategy is timeless. Make someone believe they need you more than you need them. Give them just enough to survive but never enough to thrive. Restrict their access to the tools and relationships that would allow them to function independently. And above all, never let them learn enough about the economics of the arrangement to realize they are being used. He might as well have been writing about retail mortgage banking.

This chapter covers the final three extraction methods, and I saved them for last because they are the ones that feel the most personal. The rate spread theft and the management overrides and the technology markups are all financial maneuvers that happen in the background. They are impersonal in the sense that the people perpetrating them may not even know your name. But the three methods in this chapter are different. The lead program, the marketing materials, and the non-compete clause are all designed to create a very specific emotional response in you. They are designed to make you feel like you need the company. They are designed to make you believe that without the company's leads, without the company's marketing department, and without the company's permission, you cannot survive on your own. That dependency is not an accident. It is the product.

Way Number Ten: The Lead Program That Gives You Scraps

Nearly every retail mortgage bank has some version of a lead program. The pitch goes something like this: the company invests in advertising, generates inbound leads from borrowers looking for mortgages, and distributes those leads to its loan officers. The company presents this as a major benefit of working under their umbrella. They will spend the marketing dollars and hand you the borrowers. All you have to do is close them. It sounds wonderful until you look at the economics.

The typical retail lead program distributes what I call scraps. These are leads that have already been filtered, scored, and sorted. The best leads go to the top producers or to managers who cherry-pick the highest value opportunities. What trickles down to the average loan officer is the bottom of the barrel: internet rate shoppers, refinance inquiries from borrowers who owe more than their home is worth, credit repair candidates who are twelve months away from qualifying, and people who filled out an online form at two in the morning because they could not sleep and had no real intention of applying for a mortgage. These are not leads. They are leftovers.

And the company charges you for them. Most retail lead programs include either a direct per-lead fee that gets deducted from your commission check or a wider spread on your rate sheet that effectively reduces your compensation on every deal you close, whether that deal came from a company lead or from your own referral network. The typical lead fee structure costs a loan officer between $2,400 and $7,200 per year, and the conversion rate on company-distributed leads averages between two and five percent. That means for every hundred leads the company sends you, you might close two to five of them. Compare that to the conversion rate on a warm referral from a Realtor you have worked with for years, which typically runs twenty to forty percent.

The math is devastating. You are paying thousands of dollars per year for leads that convert at a fraction of the rate of the relationships you built yourself. And those self-generated relationships, the ones you cultivated through years of lunches, open houses, co-marketing events, and late night phone calls, those relationships generate revenue that the company takes sixty to sixty-five percent of anyway. So you build the relationship, you close the deal, and the company takes the majority of the revenue while simultaneously charging you a fee for leads that rarely turn into anything.

But here is the real purpose of the lead program. It is not actually designed to help you close more loans. It is designed to make you feel like you need the company. As long as you believe that the company's lead pipeline is an essential part of your business model, you are less likely to leave. The lead program is a psychological anchor, not a business strategy. It keeps you tethered to the company by creating the illusion that you cannot generate enough business on your own. And that illusion is worth far more to the company than whatever the lead program costs to operate.

Way Number Eleven: The Marketing Mirage

The marketing department is one of the retail mortgage bank's favorite things to talk about during the recruiting process. When they are trying to get you in the door, the recruiter will tell you about the company's professional marketing team, the branded materials, the social media support, the co-branded flyers you can hand out at open houses, the email campaigns, the holiday cards, the custom landing pages, and the beautiful brand guidelines that make everything look polished and professional. It all sounds very impressive during the interview. Then you actually start using it, and you discover the truth.

The marketing materials your company provides are templates. Generic, one-size-fits-all templates that have the company's logo stamped on them in a place that is more prominent than your name. The flyers are the same flyers that every other loan officer in the company is handing out at every open house in every market in the country. The social media posts are pre-written blurbs that sound like they were generated by someone who has never actually spoken to a borrower. The email campaigns are compliance-approved drip sequences that are so bland and impersonal that your clients delete them before they finish reading the subject line.

And the cost of this marketing powerhouse? The typical retail marketing allocation costs a loan officer between $150 and $500 per month through direct deductions or overhead allocation. That is $1,800 to $6,000 per year for materials that you could produce yourself, or purchase from any number of mortgage-specific marketing platforms, for a fraction of the cost.

I want you to think about what $500 per month actually buys on the open market. For $500 per month, you could subscribe to a professional mortgage marketing platform that gives you fully customizable templates with your name, your photo, your brand, and your message. You could run targeted social media ads in your specific market area. You could hire a freelance graphic designer to create custom materials that look nothing like anyone else's because they are yours. You could invest in a professional headshot, a personal website, a video production setup for social media, and still have money left over. For the same amount of money that your company charges you for generic templates with their logo bigger than yours, you could build an entire marketing ecosystem that belongs to you, works for you, and travels with you when you leave.

But the company does not want you to do that. The company wants you using their materials, with their branding, distributed through their platforms, because that branding serves the company, not you. When a borrower receives a flyer from you at an open house, the first thing they see is the company's name and logo. The company is building its brand on the back of your relationship. You did the work to get invited to that open house. You built the relationship with that Realtor. You shook that borrower's hand and looked them in the eye. And the marketing department made sure that the materials you handed them had the company's name in a font twice the size of yours.

THE LEAD PROGRAM ECONOMICS

Annual cost vs. return on company leads vs. self-generated referrals

Metric	Company Leads	Your Own Referrals
Annual Cost to You	$2,400-$7,200/yr	$0 (your relationships)
Leads Received Per Year	200-500	50-150
Conversion Rate	2-5%	20-40%
Loans Closed from Source	4-25 loans	10-60 loans
Average Loan Amount	$275,000 (lower quality)	$375,000 (higher quality)
Your Revenue Per Loan (100 bps)	$2,750	$3,750
Cost Per Closed Loan	$288-$1,800	$0
WHO OWNS THE CLIENT?	The Company	YOU

Look at the last row of that chart. That is the line that matters more than any of the others. When a deal closes from a company lead, the company considers that client to be their client, not yours. If you leave the company, that client stays in the company's database, gets assigned to someone else, and you never hear from them again. When a deal closes from your own referral network, you built that relationship. You earned that trust. And in a true broker model, that client belongs to you because you own your own CRM, your own marketing platform, and your own brand. The company cannot take what belongs to you when everything in your business actually belongs to you.

Way Number Twelve: The Non-Compete Prison

We touched on non-competes in the last chapter when we discussed the legal department, but the non-compete deserves its own section because it is the final and most important link in the chain. It is the lock on the cage. Without the non-compete, every other extraction method in this book would be unsustainable, because loan officers would simply leave the moment they understood the math. The non-compete exists to make leaving feel dangerous, uncertain, and potentially career-ending. It is the fear that keeps you sitting at a desk that costs you $100,000 to $200,000 per year.

Here is how the non-compete trap works. On your first day at the company, buried inside a stack of onboarding paperwork, you sign a document that restricts your ability to work in the mortgage industry for a specified period after your employment ends. The typical non-compete in the mortgage industry covers a twelve to twenty-four month period within a geographic radius that ranges from twenty-five to one hundred miles. Some include a non-solicitation clause that prevents you from contacting any clients or referral partners you worked with during your time at the company. Others include a non-disclosure provision that prevents you from sharing anything about the company's business practices, compensation structures, or internal processes.

You signed it because you had to. It was not negotiable. The recruiter handed you the stack, showed you the highlighted signature lines, and told you it was standard industry paperwork. You signed it because you needed the job, because your family needed the income, and because the alternative was to walk away from a position that promised you leads, marketing support, and a competitive compensation plan. You signed it because everyone signs it. And the company counted on exactly that.

Now let me tell you what that piece of paper actually does to your financial future. The non-compete does not just prevent you from working at a competitor for twelve to twenty-four months. It prevents you from building a competitive alternative during that same period. It means you cannot start cultivating broker relationships while you are still employed. It means you cannot test the waters, cannot explore what independence looks like, cannot do the research and preparation that any responsible professional would do before making a career change. The non-compete forces you to make the decision blind, which is exactly what the company wants, because the less information you have, the scarier the jump looks.

THE MARKETING MIRAGE

What the company charges you vs. what you could build for the same money

What You Get	Company Marketing	Your Own Marketing
Monthly Cost	$150-$500/mo	$150-$500/mo
Branding	Company logo first, you second	YOUR name, YOUR brand
Customization	Templates only, pre-approved	Fully custom, your message
Social Media	Pre-written, generic posts	Targeted ads, your market
Email Campaigns	Compliance-approved drip, bland	Personal, engaging, yours
Client Data	Company owns it	YOU own it
Portability	Stays when you leave	Goes where you go
WHO DOES IT SERVE?	The Company	YOU

Same cost. Completely different outcome. For the exact same monthly investment, you could own every piece of your marketing, build a brand that belongs to you, and create assets that travel with you for the rest of your career. The company's marketing department does not exist to grow your business. It exists to grow the company's brand using your relationships as the delivery mechanism.

THE NON-COMPETE PRISON: WHAT FEAR COSTS YOU

Financial impact of staying one extra year due to non-compete fear

Scenario	Stay in Retail	Move to True Broker
Annual Production Volume	$15M	$15M
Effective Compensation	100 bps (retail)	200-275 bps (broker)
Annual Gross Income	$150,000	$300,000-$412,500
Less: Self-Paid Tech + Marketing	$0 (deducted already)	($18,000-$24,000)
Net Annual Income	$150,000	$282,000-$388,500
COST OF ONE EXTRA YEAR OF FEAR		$132,000-$238,500
COST OF FIVE YEARS OF FEAR		$660,000-$1,192,500

That chart should make you angry. Every single year that you stay in retail because you are afraid of a non-compete agreement costs you between $132,000 and $238,500. Over five years, the non-compete fear alone has a price tag of $660,000 to $1.19 million. That is not the total extraction. That is just the cost of the fear. The non-compete is worth more to the company than any other single document in your personnel file, because the production it retains through fear far exceeds anything the company spends on leads, marketing, technology, or legal fees combined.

I want to tell you about a woman named Lisa who worked for a large retail bank in the Memphis area. Lisa had been with the company for seven years and was producing about $22 million per year. She was well-liked, well-connected, and well-compensated by retail standards, earning roughly $220,000 per year. She was also miserable, because she had done the math. She knew the extraction was real. She had read her commission statements line by line and understood that she was generating close to half a million dollars in revenue and taking home less than half of it.

Lisa wanted to leave. She had been talking to an independent broker shop for three months and had a clear path to transition. But every time she got close to making the decision, she would pull out her employment agreement, read the non-compete clause, and put the paperwork back in the drawer. The non-compete said she could not work within fifty miles of her current office for eighteen months. For Lisa, that meant she could not serve the Memphis market, the market where she had built every single relationship she had, for a year and a half. It felt like a death sentence for her business.

Finally, Lisa did what I tell every loan officer to do. She talked to an employment attorney. Not a generalist lawyer who dabbles in employment law, but a specialist who had litigated non-compete disputes in her state. The attorney looked at her agreement and told her three things that changed her life. First, the geographic restriction was likely overbroad under Tennessee law. Second, moving from a retail model to a broker model was arguably a different enough business structure that the non-compete might not apply in the way the company intended. Third, and most importantly, her former employer would have to spend significant money to enforce it, and companies almost never pursue individual loan officers because the legal costs exceed whatever production they might recover.

Lisa put in her notice the following week. Her former employer did nothing. No letter from a lawyer. No cease and desist. No phone call. Nothing. Today Lisa is an independent broker producing $26 million per year and taking home over $480,000. She tells me that the eighteen months she spent being afraid of that piece of paper cost her roughly $400,000 in lost income. The non-compete was a scarecrow, and she spent a year and a half being afraid of straw.

(AGAIN, I am not an attorney. Consult an attorney to review your specific non-compete in your state)

THE COMPLETE EXTRACTION: ALL 12 WAYS

Annual cost of each extraction method on a loan officer producing $15M / 40 loans per year

#	Extraction Method	Annual Low	Annual High
1	Rate Spread Theft	$20,000	$40,000
2	Basis Point Shell Game	$30,000	$45,000
3	Management Override Tax	$12,000	$22,500
4	Regional VP Extraction	$8,000	$18,000
5	Corporate Overhead Bloat	$12,000	$24,000
6	LOS Markup	$1,200	$3,600
7	CRM Con + Data Lock-in	$600	$1,800
8	Quality Control Fees	$3,600	$9,600
9	Legal / Compliance Allocation	$6,000	$14,400
10	Lead Program Scraps	$2,400	$7,200
11	Marketing Mirage	$1,800	$6,000
12	Non-Compete Fear (opportunity cost)	$162,000	$291,000
	TOTAL DIRECT EXTRACTION (Ways 1-11)	$97,600	$192,100
	TOTAL WITH OPPORTUNITY COST (Ways 1-12)	$259,600	$483,100

There it is. All twelve methods, laid out on a single chart. The direct extraction from Ways 1 through 11 costs you between $97,600 and $192,100 per year. When you add the opportunity cost of the non-compete fear keeping you in your seat for even one additional year, the total impact ranges from $259,600 to almost half a million dollars. And that is for a single year. Multiply any of those numbers by five, by ten, by a full twenty-year career, and you begin to understand the scale of what has been taken from you.

This is not a negotiation problem. You cannot fix this by asking your branch manager for a better split. You cannot solve it with a bigger sign-on bonus, because as we showed in Chapter 3, that bonus comes with strings that cost you more than the bonus is worth. The only way to stop the extraction is to leave the system that was designed to extract from you. The only way to keep the cash is to own the business that generates it.

In Part Three of this book, we stop looking backward at what has been taken and start looking forward at what is possible. The next chapter is the most important one in this entire book, because it contains the seven questions that will tell you everything you need to know about whether your current company is working for you or whether you are working for them.

You now know all twelve ways they are taking your money. The question is: what are you going to do about it? Chapter 7 gives you the seven questions that will make the answer undeniable.

Part 3:
THE AWAKENING

Chapter 7:

THE 7 QUESTIONS
YOUR MANAGER DOESN'T WANT YOU TO ASK

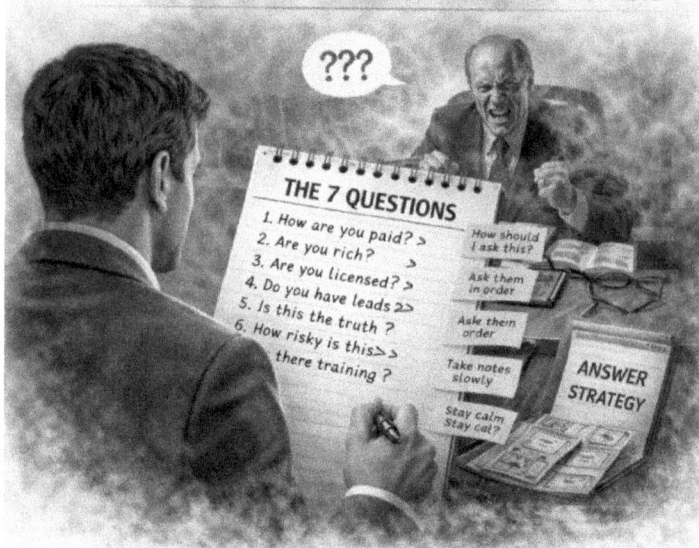

CHAPTER 7

The Seven Questions That Change Everything

The exact questions, the strategy for asking them, and what the answers reveal about your future

"Many people think they lack motivation when what they really lack is clarity. It is not always obvious when and where to take action. Some people spend their entire lives waiting for the time to be right to make an improvement."

James Clear, Atomic Habits

This is probably the most important chapter in this book. Everything before it was designed to open your eyes. Everything after it is designed to show you the path forward. But this chapter, right here, is the hinge. This is where the door swings open and you walk through it, or where you close the book and go back to sleep. I am betting on you walking through it, because if you have made it this far, you are not the kind of person who turns away from the truth.

James Clear was right when he wrote that most people do not lack motivation. They lack clarity. I have watched hundreds of loan officers sit across the table from me over the years, and the ones who stayed trapped in retail were rarely lazy or unambitious. They were some of the hardest working people I have ever met. They worked seventy-hour weeks, sacrificed weekends with their families, answered phone calls at midnight, and built referral networks that any entrepreneur would envy. What they lacked was not drive. What they lacked was a clear picture of what their employer was actually doing with the revenue they generated. The moment they got that clarity, everything changed. Not because they became different people, but because they finally had the information they needed to make a decision that matched who they already were. That is what this chapter gives you. Not motivation. Clarity.

The seven questions in this chapter are designed to be asked directly to your branch manager, your regional manager, or whoever makes the decisions about your compensation. They are simple questions. They are fair questions. Every one of them is something that any business owner would know the answer to within thirty seconds. And every one of them is a question that your company will struggle to answer honestly, because honest answers would expose the extraction that their entire business model depends on.

I need to tell you something before we get into the questions. The purpose of asking these questions is not to start a fight. The purpose is not to embarrass your manager or create conflict in your office. The purpose is to gather information. You are a business professional who generates hundreds of thousands of dollars in revenue every year, and you have every right to understand where that revenue goes. If your manager answers these questions openly and transparently, then you work for one of the rare companies that treats its loan officers with the respect they deserve. If your manager cannot answer them, will not answer them, or becomes defensive or evasive when you ask them, then you have learned something valuable about the company that controls your financial future. Either way, you win.

Question One: **"What is the total revenue generated on my average loan, from all sources, before any splits or deductions?"**

Why This Question Matters

This is the foundational question. Everything else builds on it. You cannot evaluate your compensation until you know what you are being compensated from. Most loan officers know their basis point compensation. They know they earn 100 basis points or 110 basis points or whatever their comp plan says. What most loan officers do not know is the total revenue their loan generates. The total revenue includes your basis point compensation, the lender premium or yield spread, the origination fees, the processing fees, the administrative fees, the document preparation fees, the underwriting fees, the warehouse line interest, and the servicing rights premium. When you add all of those together, the total revenue on a $375,000 loan is typically $10,500 to $15,750. Your 100 basis points gives you $3,750 of that total. The question is: where does the other $6,750 to $12,000 go?

How to Ask It

You walk into your manager's office on a Tuesday afternoon, not a Monday morning when everyone is stressed, and not a Friday afternoon when people have already checked out. Tuesday or Wednesday, mid-afternoon, when things are calm. You sit down and you say something like this: "I am trying to build a business plan for next year and I need to understand my numbers better. On my average loan, what is the total revenue the company generates from all sources? I am not asking about my split or my comp. I just want to understand the full picture of how much revenue a single loan produces."

Keep your tone curious, not confrontational. You are a professional asking a professional question. You are not accusing anyone of anything. You are gathering data for your business plan. Frame it exactly that way.

What the Answers Reveal

If your manager gives you a clear, specific number, write it down. Then go home and compare it to your compensation statement. Divide your take-home pay per loan by the total revenue number your manager gave you. That percentage is your true compensation rate. If it is under forty percent, you are being extracted from at a level that should concern you deeply. If your manager says they do not know the answer, that tells you something too. It tells you that either they genuinely do not understand the economics of their own business, which means they are not equipped to advocate for your compensation, or they do know and they do not want to tell you. Both of those answers should trouble you. If your manager gets uncomfortable, changes the subject, or tells you that information is proprietary or above your pay grade, you have your answer. A company that will not tell you how much money you generate for them is a company that is hiding something from you. Period.

Question Two: **"Can I see a complete breakdown of every fee and deduction on my commission statement, with an explanation of what each one pays for?"**

Why This Question Matters

Your commission statement is the single most important financial document in your career, and most loan officers have never read it carefully. I do not mean they have not looked at the bottom line number that gets deposited into their checking account. I mean they have never gone line by line through every deduction, fee, allocation, and adjustment to understand exactly where their money goes. The commission statement is where the extraction hides. It is where the technology markups, the management overrides, the QC fees, the marketing allocations, the E&O deductions, and the compliance charges all live. And most of them are described in language that is deliberately vague, using terms like administrative fee, processing allocation, or corporate services charge that tell you nothing about what you are actually paying for.

How to Ask It

You bring a printed copy of your most recent commission statement to the meeting. You have already highlighted every line that you do not fully understand. You set it on the desk and you say: "I have been reviewing my statements more carefully and there are a few line items I want to make sure I understand. Can we walk through these together so I can see exactly what each deduction covers?" Then you go through them one at a time. For each deduction, you ask three follow-up questions. What does this fee pay for? How is the amount calculated? And is this fee the same for every loan officer, or does it vary?

What the Answers Reveal

A transparent company will be able to explain every line on your statement in plain language. They will tell you exactly what each fee covers, how it is calculated, and whether it applies uniformly. If your manager cannot explain a specific deduction, write it down and ask them to get back to you with the answer. If they never follow up, that is your answer. The fees they cannot explain are the fees they do not want you to understand. Pay special attention to any deduction described as an allocation or an overhead charge. These are the catch-all categories that companies use to pass corporate expenses down to the people generating the revenue. When a company charges you an overhead allocation of $500 per loan and cannot tell you exactly what that $500 pays for, what they are really telling you is that they have decided you should fund their corporate infrastructure, and they do not think you deserve to know how.

"What is the total company profit margin on the loans I originate, and what percentage of revenue do I keep versus what the company retains?"

Why This Question Matters

This is the question that gets to the heart of the extraction. You already know what you earn. Question One told you the total revenue. Now you need to know the split. Not the split they put in your comp plan, which only accounts for your basis point compensation as a percentage of the loan amount. The real split. Total dollars to you divided by total dollars the loan generates. When you express the math this way, the illusion collapses. Your 100 basis points that sounded like a reasonable compensation turns out to be twenty-eight to thirty-five percent of the total revenue your loan produces. The company keeps sixty-five to seventy-two percent. And a significant portion of what the company retains is pure profit, not cost.

How to Ask It

This question requires a lighter touch because you are asking the company to reveal its profit margin, and most companies consider that information sensitive. Frame it around industry benchmarks rather than a demand for proprietary data. You say something like: "I have been reading some industry analysis that suggests the typical retail mortgage bank retains sixty to seventy percent of per-loan revenue. Does that sound about right for our company, or are we structured differently?" By citing an industry range, you are showing that you have done your homework and you are giving your manager a chance to either confirm the range or differentiate the company from it. Either response gives you information.

What the Answers Reveal

If your manager confirms that the company retains in that range, you now have the number you need to calculate your annual extraction. Multiply the company's retained percentage by your total annual revenue, and that is the amount of money you generated that someone else keeps. If your manager says the company's retention is lower than the industry average, ask them to show you the math. A company that genuinely retains less than its competitors should be proud to prove it. If your manager says they do not know the company's margin, deflects to a different topic, or tells you that profit margins are a corporate-level metric that does not apply to individual loan officers, recognize that answer for what it is. They are telling you that the company's profitability is not your concern. But since your labor is the primary source of that profitability, it absolutely is your concern.

Question Four: "If I leave this company, what happens to my client database, my CRM records, and my referral partner contact information?"

Why This Question Matters

Your book of business is the most valuable asset you own as a loan officer. It is more valuable than your production numbers, more valuable than your industry certifications, and more valuable than any sign-on bonus any recruiter will ever offer you. Your book of business is the accumulated result of every relationship you have built over the course of your career. The answer to this question tells you whether you own that asset or whether the company owns it. And if the company owns it, then you are building wealth for someone else every time you add a contact, log a phone call, or send a follow-up email.

How to Ask It

This question is easier to frame naturally because it does not sound adversarial. You say: "I have been thinking about how to better organize my referral partners and past clients. Before I put a bunch of time into updating the CRM, I want to make sure I understand our data policies. If someone were to leave the company, would they be able to export their contacts, or does that data stay with the company?" Notice you are not asking about yourself specifically. You are asking about the company's data policy in general. That makes it feel less like a threat and more like an innocent operational question. But the answer will tell you everything you need to know about whether your years of relationship-building belong to you or to the company.

What the Answers Reveal

There are really only two possible answers to this question, and both of them are revealing. If the company says you can export your data, ask them to show you how. Ask to see the export process in writing. If it exists, that is a good sign, but it is rare. Most retail mortgage banks do not allow data exports for departing employees. If the company says the data stays with the company, you now know that every contact you add to the CRM is a contact you are handing to your employer. You are building their database with your relationships, and the day you leave, those relationships become their asset. The practical implication is this: if you cannot take your data with you, you need to start building a parallel system outside the company's infrastructure. A personal spreadsheet, a personal CRM, a personal contact list that lives on your own computer and belongs to you. Because the relationships you built belong to you morally, even if the company has structured the technology to claim them legally.

Question Five: **"How many people in the company are compensated, directly or through overrides, from the loans I originate?"**

Why This Question Matters

Chapter 4 of this book laid out the management pyramid in detail, showing how branch managers, area managers, regional VPs, and divisional SVPs all collect basis point overrides on every loan you close. This question forces the company to quantify the pyramid. Most loan officers have no idea how many people are paid from their production, because the company deliberately keeps that information compartmentalized. Your branch manager knows their override, but they may not know the regional VP's override. The regional VP knows their number but may not know the divisional structure above them. By asking for the total count, you are asking the company to map the extraction chain from top to bottom.

How to Ask It

Frame this one around curiosity about the company's support structure. You say: "I have been thinking about all the people who support the loan process from start to finish. Between management, operations, compliance, underwriting, and corporate, how many people would you estimate are directly or indirectly compensated from a single loan that I originate?" This framing works because it sounds like admiration for the company's infrastructure rather than a complaint about the cost of that infrastructure. Let your manager talk. They will probably undercount at first, because they will think of the direct participants like the processor and the underwriter. Then gently expand the question: "And what about the management layers? I know you have an override, and there are people above you in the org chart. How many levels of management get paid from each deal?"

What the Answers Reveal

The typical retail mortgage bank has seven to twelve people who receive some form of compensation from each loan an individual officer originates. That includes the branch manager, the area manager, the regional VP, the processing staff, the underwriting department, the compliance team, and the corporate overhead allocation that funds executive compensation. If your manager gives you a number under five, they are either unaware of the management override structure above them or they are being selective with the truth. If they give you a number in the seven to twelve range, ask a follow-up: "And what does each of those layers cost in total per loan?" The answer to that question will either confirm the extraction or expose the company's unwillingness to discuss it.

Question Six: **"What is the actual cost to the company for the technology, marketing, and compliance services that are deducted from my compensation?"**

Why This Question Matters

Chapters 5 and 6 documented the technology markups, the CRM con, the marketing mirage, and the compliance fee stack in detail. This question asks the company to do what those chapters did: compare what they charge you for these services to what the services actually cost. The gap between the company's cost and your deduction is pure markup, and that markup is extraction by another name. A company that charges you $325 per month for an LOS that costs $65 per month is not providing you a service. They are using a mandatory tool as a revenue center.

How to Ask It

This is the most sensitive question on the list because it directly challenges the company's pricing on internal services. Frame it as a cost comparison exercise. You say: "I have been looking at ways to reduce my overhead and increase my net income. I wanted to ask about our technology costs specifically. What does the company pay per user for our LOS license? And is the amount I see deducted on my statement the same as what the company pays, or is there a markup to cover support and integration?" The key phrase is "markup to cover support and integration." You are giving the company an opportunity to explain the gap. If they take that opportunity and provide a reasonable justification, listen to it carefully and evaluate whether the explanation holds water. If they refuse to tell you what the company pays for the technology, you have learned that the pricing is not defensible.

What the Answers Reveal

If the company tells you there is no markup, ask them to prove it. Request a copy of the vendor invoice or the enterprise contract pricing. A company with nothing to hide will have no problem showing you. If the company admits there is a markup but justifies it as covering internal support, integration, and maintenance, do the math. A reasonable support markup on a $65 per month

LOS license might be twenty to thirty percent, bringing the total to $78 to $85 per month. If you are being charged $325 per month, that is not a support markup. That is a three hundred percent margin on a captive customer. If your manager cannot or will not tell you what the company pays for the tools it charges you for, the silence is your answer. You are being overcharged, and the company knows that transparency would expose the overcharge.

Question Seven: **"If I were to leave this company and become an independent broker, what specific services would I lose that I could not replace on the open market for less money?"**

Why This Question Matters

This is the question that makes everything real. The first six questions are about understanding the extraction. This question is about understanding the alternative. It forces the company to make its case for why you should stay, and it forces that case to be specific and verifiable. The company cannot answer this question with vague platitudes about culture, brand recognition, or team environment. Those things have value, but they do not have a dollar value that justifies a six-figure annual extraction. This question demands a concrete, economic answer: what do you provide that is worth more than what you charge for it?

How to Ask It

You do not have to frame this one delicately, because by the time you ask it, your manager already knows where this conversation is going. But you can still keep it professional and respectful. You say: "I want to be straightforward with you. I have been doing a lot of research on the broker model, and the economics look significantly different from what I am experiencing here. Before I make any decisions, I want to give this company a fair chance to make its case. If I left and went independent, what specific things would I lose that I could not find somewhere else? Not feelings or culture. I am talking about services, technology, support, and economics. What makes this company worth the difference in compensation?"

Then be quiet. Let the silence work. Do not fill it. Do not help your manager answer. Do not suggest possibilities. Just wait, and let them build their case from scratch.

What the Answers Reveal

This question is the moment of truth, and I have heard every possible response over the years. Some managers will list the technology stack, the compliance infrastructure, the processing support, and the underwriting team. If they do, you already have the data from Chapters 5 and 6 to calculate whether those services are priced at market rates or at inflated rates. Some managers will talk about the company's brand and the trust it builds with borrowers and referral partners. That is a legitimate point, but you should ask yourself whether the brand is more valuable than your personal reputation. If your Realtors send you business because they trust the company name or because they trust you, the answer to that question tells you whether the brand is worth what it costs. Some managers will talk about the lead program. You know from Chapter 6 what those leads are worth. Some will get emotional and talk about loyalty, team spirit, and how much the company has invested in you. That is not an economic argument. That is a retention pitch.

And some managers, the honest ones, will look you in the eye and say something like: "I understand why you are asking, and I am not sure I can make a case that beats the math." Those are the managers worth respecting, because they are telling you the truth. They are trapped in the same system you are, and they know it. When you encounter that kind of honesty, honor it. Thank them for being straight with you. And then go build something that works for both of you, because some of the best broker partnerships I have seen started with a retail manager who had the courage to be honest.

THE SEVEN QUESTIONS SCORECARD

Score each question based on the response you receive

#	Question Topic	GREEN: Transparent	YELLOW: Vague	RED: Refused / Hostile
1	Total revenue per loan	Gave a clear number	Said "it varies"	Said proprietary
2	Commission statement breakdown	Explained every line	Skipped some items	Would not review
3	Company profit margin / retention %	Shared the split	Gave a range	Deflected entirely
4	Client data / CRM ownership	You can export	"We will discuss"	Data stays, period
5	Number of people paid per loan	Gave a count of 7+	Said "a few"	Said not your concern
6	Actual cost of tech / services	Showed vendor cost	Admitted some markup	Refused to disclose
7	What you would lose going broker	Gave specific answers	Said "everything"	Got angry or threatened

HOW TO READ YOUR SCORE

Tally your results and evaluate what they mean for your future

Your Results	What It Means
5-7 GREEN	You work for a transparent company. You may still benefit from the broker model economically, but your employer respects you enough to tell you the truth. That is rare and worth acknowledging.
3-4 GREEN, rest YELLOW	Your company is partially transparent. They answer the easy questions but get evasive on the ones that matter most. The vagueness is not accidental. Start doing the math on your own and compare your true compensation to the broker alternative.
3+ RED	Your company is actively hiding the economics of your employment from you. The refusal to answer fair, reasonable questions about your own compensation is a bright red flag. The extraction is real, it is significant, and the company knows that transparency would expose it. It is time to explore your options seriously.
5+ RED	You do not work for a company. You work for an extraction machine. Every dollar you generate is being filtered through a system designed to keep you in the dark about how much of it you are losing. This is not a conversation about career optimization. This is a conversation about financial survival. Chapter 9 is written for you.

I want to close this chapter by telling you what happened when I asked these questions at the retail bank where I spent the early part of my career. I did not have all seven questions back then. I only had three. I asked about the total revenue per loan. I asked about the management overrides. And I asked what I would lose if I went independent. My manager at the time was a good man. He was not malicious or deceptive by nature. He was a company man who believed in the system because the system had been good to him. He answered my first question with a number that turned out to be roughly accurate, and that number was the one that started the cascade. When I compared it to my compensation, the math did not work. He struggled with the second question about overrides and eventually admitted that there were several layers above him that he was not fully aware of. And when I asked the third question about going independent, he paused for a long time and then said something I will never forget. He said: "Michael, if you can figure out how to do this on your own, you probably should."

That was not the answer the company would have wanted him to give. It was the answer of a man who saw the math the same way I did and had enough integrity to admit it. I respected him for that then, and I respect him for it now. That conversation was the beginning of the path that eventually led me to Edge Home Finance, to complete transparency, and to the conviction that every loan officer in America deserves to know exactly where their money goes.

You have the seven questions now. You have the strategy for asking each one. You know what the answers mean, and you know what the non-answers mean. The only thing left is whether you will actually ask them. I cannot do that part for you. But I can tell you this: every loan officer who has asked these questions and acted on the answers has told me the same thing. They all said it was the most important conversation of their career. Not because the answers were surprising. Because the answers finally gave them permission to do what they already knew they needed to do.

Go ask the questions. Then come back and read Chapter 8, because once you have the answers, you are going to need a plan.

Visit keepthecash.com to download a printable version of the Seven Questions Scorecard and the Keep The Cash Calculator to see exactly what your numbers would look like as an independent broker.

Chapter 8:
THE CEO LOAN OFFICER

CHAPTER 8

The CEO Loan Officer

You are already running a business. You just do not get paid like it.

"As long as you are alive, you will either live to accomplish your own goals and dreams or be used as a resource to accomplish someone else's."

Grant Cardone, The 10X Rule

I want you to do something for me right now. I want you to think about what you did last Tuesday. Not the big moments. The small ones. Think about the first hour of your day. You probably checked your phone before your feet hit the floor, scrolling through emails from borrowers, text messages from Realtors, and rate alerts from your LOS. You got dressed and drove to the office or sat down at your home desk and started returning calls. You followed up on three pre-approvals. You checked the status of two loans in underwriting. You called a title company about a closing that was supposed to happen on Friday. You had lunch with a Realtor who sends you four or five deals a year, and during that lunch, you talked about market conditions, interest rate trends, and which neighborhoods are moving. After lunch you took two new applications, ran credit on both, and priced three loan scenarios for a borrower who wanted to compare a thirty-year fixed against an ARM. You spent forty-five minutes on the phone with a nervous first-time buyer who had questions about closing costs. You responded to sixteen emails. You updated your pipeline. And somewhere around six or seven in the evening, you finally stopped working. Now I want you to look at that day and tell me what part of it was the work of an employee.

None of it. Every single task you performed that day was the work of a business owner. You generated your own leads through relationships you built. You managed your own pipeline. You consulted with clients on complex financial products. You marketed yourself over lunch. You negotiated timelines with vendors. You problem-solved on the fly when underwriting came back with conditions. You managed your own time, set your own priorities, and made dozens of independent decisions that directly affected your income. There was no manager standing over your shoulder telling you which calls to make or which emails to answer first. You ran your day the way a CEO runs a company, because that is exactly what you are. You are a CEO who has been misclassified as an employee, and that misclassification is costing you a fortune.

Grant Cardone built a real estate empire worth billions of dollars, and he did it by refusing to accept the idea that someone else should determine his financial ceiling. When he wrote that you will either accomplish your own goals or be used as a resource to accomplish someone else's, he was describing the exact choice that every retail loan officer faces whether they realize it or not. You are a resource. You are arguably the most valuable resource in the entire retail mortgage operation. Without you, there are no loans. Without loans, there is no revenue. Without revenue, the branch manager has no override, the regional VP has no bonus, and the corporate office has no profit margin. You are the engine of the entire machine, and the machine pays you like a part-time mechanic.

This chapter is about the mindset shift that changes everything. It is not about learning new skills, because you already have the skills. It is not about working harder, because you already work harder than most people in any industry. It is about seeing yourself differently. It is about recognizing that the work you do every single day is the work of a business owner, and then making the decision to get paid like one.

The CEO Job Description You Already Fulfill

If I wrote a job description for the CEO of a small financial services company, it would look something like this. The CEO is responsible for client acquisition through personal networking and relationship development. The CEO manages a pipeline of complex financial transactions from origination through closing. The CEO provides expert consultation to clients on a range of financial products and regulatory requirements. The CEO develops and maintains strategic partnerships with real estate professionals, financial planners, attorneys, and other referral sources. The CEO manages vendor relationships with title companies, appraisers, insurance providers, and settlement agents. The CEO is responsible for marketing, branding, and business development activities. The CEO ensures regulatory compliance across all transactions. And the CEO is accountable for all revenue generation.

Read that again slowly. Every single line in that job description is something you already do. You are not doing some of those things. You are doing all of them. You are the CEO, the sales team, the marketing department, the client services manager, the compliance officer, and the business development director all rolled into one person. The only thing you are not doing is collecting the revenue that a CEO of a business that size would collect, because your company has structured the arrangement so that they collect the majority of that revenue and hand you back a fraction of it with a label that says compensation.

CEO FUNCTIONS YOU ALREADY PERFORM

Every role of a business owner mapped to your daily work as a loan officer

CEO Function	What a CEO Does	What YOU Already Do
Sales & Revenue	Generates all company revenue through client relationships	Generate 100% of your production through your own relationships
Marketing	Builds brand, creates awareness, attracts new clients	Attend open houses, host events, build Realtor networks, run social media
Client Services	Manages client experience from first contact to delivery	Guide borrowers from pre-qual through closing, handle every question and concern
Partnerships	Develops strategic alliances with complementary businesses	Build referral networks with Realtors, builders, financial planners, attorneys
Vendor Management	Negotiates and manages third-party service providers	Coordinate with title companies, appraisers, insurance agents, inspectors
Compliance	Ensures all operations meet regulatory standards	Maintain licensing, follow TRID, RESPA, ECOA, and state regulations on every deal

Pipeline Mgmt	Manages workflow, production schedules, and delivery timelines	Track every loan from application to closing, manage conditions, meet deadlines
Financial Consulting	Provides expert guidance on complex financial decisions	Advise borrowers on loan programs, rate structures, down payment strategies, DTI
YOUR PAY	CEO of a company doing $490K in revenue: $300K-$400K+	You: $150K-$180K (28-35% of the revenue you create)

That last row is the one I want burned into your memory. A CEO who runs a financial services business generating $490,000 in annual revenue would expect to take home $300,000 to $400,000 or more, depending on the overhead structure. You run that exact business. You perform every function on that chart. And you take home $150,000 to $180,000 because someone convinced you that you are an employee and employees get a fraction of what they produce. You are not an employee. You are a CEO who has been conditioned to accept an employee's paycheck.

The Three Lies That Keep You Thinking Like an Employee

The retail mortgage industry has spent decades perfecting three specific lies that prevent loan officers from seeing themselves as business owners. These lies are woven into the culture, the language, and the compensation structure of every retail bank in the country, and they are so deeply embedded that most loan officers accept them as truth without ever questioning them.

Lie Number One: You need the company's infrastructure to close loans. This is the foundational lie, and it is the one the company invests the most energy in maintaining. The message is simple: you could never do this on your own because you do not have access to underwriting, processing, compliance, technology, and investor relationships. Without the company's infrastructure, you would be lost. This lie works because it contains a grain of truth. You do need infrastructure. You need an LOS, a CRM, a pricing engine, compliance support, and investor relationships. What the company does not want you to know is that all of that infrastructure is available on the open market at a fraction of what they charge you for it. In a true broker model, you can access every piece of infrastructure you need through third-party vendors who compete for your business. You are not choosing between the company's infrastructure and nothing. You are choosing between the company's overpriced, proprietary infrastructure and a marketplace of competitive alternatives that cost less and often perform better.

Lie Number Two: Your income will go down if you leave. This lie is the one your manager tells you when you start asking the seven questions from Chapter 7. The pitch goes something like this: sure, brokers have higher splits, but they also have higher expenses, and when you factor in all the costs of running your own shop, you end up making about the same or less. This is mathematically false, and we have proven it with actual numbers throughout this book. The typical retail loan officer producing $18 million in annual volume earns $150,000 to $180,000 after all deductions. The same loan officer in a true broker model, using a transparent compensation structure like the 2.75% model at Edge Home Finance, earns $300,000 to $471,000 on the same volume after paying for all of their own technology, marketing, and overhead at market rates. The income does not go down. It doubles, and in many cases it nearly triples. The company knows this, which is exactly why they work so hard to make sure you never see the comparison.

Lie Number Three: Being a broker is risky and unstable. This is the fear lie, and it is the most insidious of the three because it targets your family. The message is that the retail bank provides stability, benefits, and security that you would lose as an independent broker. The company wants you to picture yourself alone in a home office with no safety net, no health insurance, no retirement plan, and no guaranteed income. But let me ask you something. How stable is a job where you eat what you kill? You are already one hundred percent commission. Your company does not pay you a salary. If you do not close loans, you do not earn money. That is already the risk profile of a business owner. The only difference is that a business owner gets to keep the revenue. You take all the risk of an entrepreneur and receive the compensation of an employee. That is not stability. That is the illusion of stability, and the company charges you between $100,000 and $200,000 per year for that illusion.

THE MINDSET SHIFT: EMPLOYEE vs. CEO LOAN OFFICER

How you think determines how you get paid

Area	Employee Mindset	CEO Mindset
Compensation	"My comp plan is 100 bps"	"I generate $490K in revenue. What percentage do I keep?"
Technology	"The company provides my tools"	"What do these tools cost, and can I buy them for less?"
Marketing	"The company handles marketing"	"Whose brand are they building with my relationships?"
Client Data	"My contacts are in the CRM"	"Who owns that data when I leave?"
Risk	"At least I have a stable job"	"I am 100% commission. I already carry all the risk."
Fees	"Those are just the cost of doing business"	"Every hidden fee is money I earned and someone else took"
Career Path	"Maybe I will get promoted to manager"	"I already run this business. I just need to own it."
Non-Compete	"I cannot leave because of my agreement"	"A piece of paper is not worth $200K per year of my family's future"

Read the left column out loud and then read the right column out loud. Listen to the difference. The left column sounds like someone who has accepted the rules of a game they did not design. The right column sounds like someone who has realized they are the game. The shift from the left column to the right column is not a career change. It is a perspective change. And perspective is the most valuable thing you can own in this industry, because the moment you see yourself as the CEO of your own financial services company, every decision you make from that point forward changes.

The Revenue You Actually Generate

Let me put real numbers on the CEO Loan Officer concept, because this section needs to land with the force of a sledgehammer. I am going to walk you through the total economic value you create for your company, and I am going to compare it to what you actually receive. These numbers are based on an average producing loan officer at $18 million in annual volume, closing approximately 48 loans per year at an average loan amount of $375,000.

The total revenue generated on a single loan includes the origination income, the lender premium or yield spread, the processing and administrative fees, and the servicing rights value. On a $375,000 loan, that total ranges from $10,200 to $15,750 depending on the company's rate sheet structure and investor relationships. Using a conservative midpoint of $10,200 per loan, your 40 annual loans generate $489,600 in total revenue for the company. Using the higher end of $15,750 per loan, you generate $756,000. Either way, you are responsible for creating roughly half a million to three quarters of a million dollars in annual revenue.

Your take-home compensation on 40 loans at 100 basis points on $375,000 per loan is $150,000 before any deductions. After the technology fees, the CRM charges, the marketing allocations, the E&O deductions, and the per-loan fees that we documented in Chapters 5 and 6, your net take-home is typically $150,000 to $165,000. That means you are keeping somewhere between twenty-two and thirty-four percent of the total revenue you generate. The company keeps the rest.

YOUR TRUE VALUE vs. YOUR TRUE PAY

Annual revenue you create compared to what you actually take home

Revenue Line Item	Conservative	High End
LO Origination Income (100 bps x 40 loans)	$150,000	$180,000
Secondary Market Rates	$139,200	$315,600
Processing & Admin Fees (per loan)	$50,400	$81,600
Servicing Rights Value	$120,000	$178,800
TOTAL ANNUAL REVENUE YOU GENERATE	$459,600	$756,000
Less: Your Net Take-Home After All Deductions	$150,000	$165,000
COMPANY RETAINS	$309,600	$591,000
YOUR SHARE OF REVENUE YOU CREATED	32.6%	23.8%

Read that bottom row one more time. You keep between 23.8% and 32.6% of the revenue you create. The company keeps between 67.4% and 77.2%. And you are the one who generated every single dollar of it. No loan officer walked into that company and said, "I would like to produce half a million dollars in revenue this year and keep about a fifth of it." Nobody would agree to those terms if they were stated that clearly. But because the compensation is expressed in basis points rather than percentages of total revenue, and because the deductions and extractions are spread across a dozen different line items and overhead allocations, the true split remains invisible to the people who deserve to see it most.

What Your P&L Looks Like as a CEO

If you took the same $15 million in production and ran it through a true broker model at 2.75% transparent compensation, your revenue picture changes dramatically. The math is straightforward. On $15 million at 2.75%, your gross compensation is $412,500. Now let us subtract every legitimate business expense you would have as an independent broker operating at market rates.

Your LOS license costs $75 per month, or $900 per year. Your CRM costs $100 per month, or $1,200 per year. Your pricing engine costs $50 per month, or $600 per year. Your marketing budget, which you control and direct entirely toward building your own brand, runs $500 per month, or $6,000 per year. Your compliance and licensing costs run about $3,600 per year. Your E&O insurance is $1,200 per year. Your processing costs, whether you hire a processor or use a processing service, run about $500 to $750 per loan, or $24,000 to $36,000 per year. Your office overhead, whether you rent a small space or work from home, averages $6,000 to $12,000 per year. Health insurance, which the retail company was not providing anyway since you were a 1099 contractor or commission-only W-2, runs $8,400 to $18,000 per year for a family plan depending on your state and the coverage you select.

Add all of that up and your total operating expenses as a CEO Loan Officer range from $51,900 to $79,500 per year. Subtract that from your $333,000 gross compensation and your net income as an independent broker is $333,000 to $443,100. Compare that to your net income in retail of $150,000 to $165,000. The difference is $183,000 per year. Over a ten-year career, that is $1.83 million. Over twenty years, that is $3.66 million.

THE CEO LOAN OFFICER P&L

Your annual income in retail vs. as a CEO broker on $18M volume

Line Item	Retail Employee	CEO Broker
Gross Compensation	$180,000	$495,000
Technology (LOS, CRM, Pricing Engine)	(Deducted already)	($2,700)
Marketing (YOUR brand, YOUR tools)	(Deducted already)	($6,000)
Processing Costs ($500-$750/loan)	(Deducted already)	($24,000-$36,000)
Compliance, Licensing, E&O	(Deducted already)	($4,800)
Office Overhead	(Deducted already)	($6,000-$12,000)
Health Insurance (family plan)	(Not provided)	($8,400-$18,000)
Total Operating Expenses	(Hidden in your split)	($51,900-$79,500)
Retail Hidden Deductions (Tech, QC, Mktg, Legal)	($15,000-$30,000)	$0
NET ANNUAL INCOME	$150,000-$165,000	$415,500-$443,100
10-YEAR CAREER EARNINGS	$1.5M-$1.65M	$4.15M-$4.43M

Stare at that chart until it sinks in. Same loan officer. Same volume. Same borrowers. Same Realtors. Same work ethic. Same sixty-hour weeks. The only thing that changes is the economic structure around you. In retail, you net $150,000 to $165,000. As a CEO Loan Officer in a true broker model, you net $415,500 to $443,100. The gap is not a rounding error. It is not a minor improvement. It is a complete transformation of your financial life, and it is available to you right now if you are willing to make the shift from thinking like an employee to thinking like an owner.

I want to tell you about a couple named Derek and Karen who both worked as loan officers at the same retail bank in Nashville. They were married to each other and between the two of them they produced about $34 million per year. Combined retail income: roughly $340,000. Good money by any standard, and they were grateful for it. They had four kids, a nice house in Franklin, and a life that looked comfortable from the outside.

Derek read an early draft of this book. He did the math on a Tuesday night after the kids were in bed, using the same formulas you have seen in these pages. When Karen came downstairs and found him at the kitchen table with a calculator and a legal pad, she asked what he was working on. He turned the legal pad around so she could read it. At the top, he had written their combined retail income: $340,000. Below that, he had calculated their combined income in a true broker model at 2.75%: $935,000. Below that, he had written a single sentence: "We are leaving $595,000 on the table every year."

Karen sat down. They talked until two in the morning. They ran the numbers again. They calculated their expenses. They called an employment attorney the next day about their non-competes. Three months later, they moved their licenses. Their first full year as independent brokers, their combined income was $867,000. Not quite the $935,000 on the legal pad, because they were still building some of their systems. But $867,000 is a long way from $340,000. Derek told me that the only thing he regrets is not doing it five years earlier, because that delay cost them nearly $3 million.

You do not need to become a different person to make this shift. You do not need to learn new skills, change your work habits, or reinvent your career. You need to see yourself clearly. You are already the CEO. The only thing left is claiming the title and collecting the pay that comes with it.

Now that you see yourself as the CEO, Chapter 9 shows you the vehicle that makes it real: the true broker model. Not the old broker model that gave the channel a bad name. The new one. The transparent one. The one that is cheaper, faster, and easier.

Part 4:

KEEP THE CASH

RETAIL MORTGAGE BANKER
EXIT
LOAN OFFICER
MORTGAGE BROKER
INDEPENDENT & FREE
✓ LOWER RATES!
✓ MORE LENDERS!

Chapter 9:
THE TRUE BROKER ADVANTAGE

CHAPTER 9

The True Broker Advantage

Real numbers. Cheaper, faster, easier. Why the true broker model with complete transparency is the future of the mortgage industry.

"Understanding what is true is essential for success, and being radically transparent about everything, including mistakes and weaknesses, helps create the understanding that leads to improvements."

Ray Dalio, Principles: Life and Work

I need to clear something up before we go any further, because the word "broker" carries baggage in this industry and I do not want that baggage weighing down a single page of this chapter. When most loan officers hear the word broker, they think of the late 1990s and early 2000s, back when some brokers operated like the Wild West of mortgage lending. Stated income loans. No-doc programs. Yield spread premiums that borrowers never understood. Some brokers back then did things that were flat-out wrong, and the Dodd-Frank Act of 2010 cleaned house in ways that needed to happen. I am not here to defend any of that, and I am not here to resurrect it. What I am here to tell you is that the true broker model of today is nothing like what existed twenty years ago, and the people who want you to stay in retail banking are counting on you confusing the two.

The true broker model I am describing in this chapter is built on a foundation that would make Ray Dalio proud: radical transparency. Every dollar visible. Every fee explained. Every basis point accounted for. No hidden revenue streams, no buried overrides, no back-end servicing profits that the loan officer never sees. The true broker model operates on the principle that when you show people exactly where the money goes, good things happen. The loan officer earns more. The borrower pays less. The transaction moves faster. And trust, which is the most valuable currency in any business relationship, grows instead of erodes.

This chapter is going to lay out the true broker advantage with real numbers, side-by-side comparisons, and the kind of transparency that retail banks would rather you never see. By the time you finish reading, you will understand exactly why the true broker model is cheaper for borrowers, faster to close, easier to operate, and more profitable for loan officers. And you will understand why it is not just an alternative to retail banking. It is the future of this industry.

Cheaper: Why Borrowers Pay Less Through a True Broker

Let me start with the borrower, because if the model is not better for the borrower then nothing else matters. The entire mortgage industry exists to serve people who need financing to buy or refinance homes, and any business model that fails to serve them well does not deserve to survive regardless of how much money it makes for the people inside it. The good news is that the true broker model does not just match retail pricing for borrowers. It beats it, and it beats it consistently.

Here is why. A retail mortgage bank is a vertically integrated operation. It originates the loan, underwrites the loan, funds the loan, and in many cases services the loan. Every layer of that vertical integration adds cost. The underwriting department has overhead. The funding department has overhead. The servicing department has overhead. The corporate office that manages all of those departments has overhead. The regional managers who oversee the branch managers who oversee the loan officers have overhead. Every single layer of that structure has to be paid for, and it all gets paid for out of the revenue generated on your borrower's loan.

A true broker does not carry any of that vertical overhead. The broker originates the loan and then sends it to a wholesale lender who underwrites, funds, and services it. The wholesale lender operates at massive scale, processing thousands of loans per month with highly automated systems that drive per-loan costs far below what any retail bank can achieve. Because the wholesale lender's costs are lower, the wholesale rate sheets are consistently better than the retail rate sheets. This is not an opinion and it is not a marketing claim. It is a structural economic reality that has been confirmed by every major industry study conducted in the last decade.

BORROWER PRICING: RETAIL BANK vs. TRUE BROKER

Same borrower, same credit profile, same day - real pricing comparison on a $400,000 loan

Pricing Element	Retail Bank	True Broker
30-Year Fixed Rate (Same Day)	6.5%	5.500%
Origination Fee	1.00% ($4,000)	1.00% ($4,000)
Lender/Admin Fees	$1,250 - $2,500	$1195
Processing Fee	$600 - $1000	$0
Monthly Payment (P&I)	$2,528	$2,271
Monthly Savings for Borrower	--	$257/month
Lifetime Savings (30 years)	--	$92,520

This rate advantage is not a one-time anomaly. Industry data consistently shows that wholesale rates run 25 to 75 basis points below retail rates on comparable products, depending on the day, the loan program, and the investor. On a $400,000 loan, the basis point advantage saves the borrower $257 per month and $92,520 over the life of the loan. On larger loan amounts, the savings scale proportionally. A $600,000 loan saves the borrower roughly $386 per month and more than $138,960 over thirty years. These are not hypothetical projections. These are the mathematical results of removing the layers of overhead that retail banks build into every rate they quote.

And here is the part that should make you angry if you work in retail. Your borrower is paying a higher rate, and you are not the one benefiting from that higher rate. The extra revenue generated by the retail markup flows to the company, not to you. The borrower pays more, you earn less, and the only winner is the corporate structure sitting between you and the wholesale market. In a true broker model, the borrower pays less and you earn more, because the overhead that inflated the retail price and suppressed your compensation has been removed from the equation entirely.

Faster: Why Broker Loans Close Quicker

Speed matters in real estate. Every loan officer knows the frustration of losing a deal because underwriting took too long, or because the file got stuck in a queue behind two hundred other loans at a retail bank that was short-staffed in the operations department. Every Realtor has a horror story about a buyer who lost a house because the lender could not close on time. Speed is not a luxury in this business. It is a competitive weapon, and the true broker model gives you a sharper one.

When you work for a retail bank, you have one underwriting department. If that department is backed up, your loans wait. If they are short-staffed because someone quit or got transferred, your loans wait longer. If corporate decides to implement a new system or change a process mid-quarter, your loans get caught in the transition. You have zero control over the operational speed of the company that processes your loans, and yet your reputation with borrowers and Realtors depends entirely on that speed.

In the true broker model, you are not locked into a single lender's operation. You submit your loans to wholesale lenders who compete for your business, and that competition extends to turn times. If Lender A is running 21-day underwriting turns and Lender B is running 14-day turns on the same product, you send the file to Lender B. If Lender C has a dedicated rush lane for purchase transactions and can get you a clear-to-close in ten days, you send the purchase deals there. You are not a captive of one company's operational capacity. You are a free agent with access to dozens of wholesale lenders who are actively competing to earn your submission by offering better rates, better service, and faster closings.

CLOSING SPEED: RETAIL vs. TRUE BROKER

Average turn times from application to clear-to-close

Timeline Metric	Retail Bank	True Broker
Avg. Days to Clear-to-Close	25-38 days	11-23 days
Number of Lenders Available	1 (your employer)	150+ wholesale lenders
Ability to Shop Turn Times	None	Full flexibility
Rush/Priority Lanes	At company discretion	Available at multiple lenders
Backup Lender if File Gets Stuck	None - start over with a different company	Move file to another lender
Impact on Realtor Confidence	"Hope we close on time"	"We WILL close on time"

That last row is worth its weight in gold, and I mean that literally. The difference between a Realtor who hopes you can close on time and a Realtor who knows you will close on time is the difference between getting three referrals a year and getting twelve. When you can look a Realtor in the eye and say that you have access to dozens of lenders and that if one of them gets slow you will move the file to another one without missing the closing date, you become the most valuable lending partner that Realtor has ever worked with. You become the person they call first on every deal. And every additional referral that comes through that confidence is revenue that the broker model made possible.

Easier: Why the True Broker Model Is Simpler to Operate

This is the one that surprises most retail loan officers when they first hear it, because the conventional wisdom in the industry says that going independent means taking on a mountain of complexity. You will have to manage your own compliance, find your own technology, handle your own processing, and navigate a jungle of wholesale lender relationships. That is the story retail banks tell, and it is designed to make independence sound overwhelming. The reality is the opposite.

Twenty years ago, there was some truth to the complexity argument. Setting up shop as an independent broker in 2005 meant cobbling together a patchwork of systems, negotiating individual agreements with every lender, and managing compliance largely on your own. But the wholesale mortgage market in 2026 is a completely different landscape. Technology has automated the hard parts. Wholesale lenders have streamlined their submission processes. Broker platforms have consolidated pricing, compliance, and lender management into single portals that are easier to use than most retail LOS systems. The infrastructure that used to require a team of people to manage can now be operated by one loan officer with a laptop and a phone.

At Edge Home Finance, for example, the true broker model is designed specifically to remove complexity rather than add it. Compensation is set at a flat 2.75% with total transparency, which means you never have to calculate your effective split or wonder where the rest of the revenue went. Pricing comes through a single portal that aggregates rates from dozens of wholesale lenders in real time, so instead of being locked into one rate sheet, you can comparison shop across the entire market in sixty seconds. Compliance is managed at the company level, so your licensing, your disclosures, and your regulatory obligations are handled through systems that are already built and already tested.

Processing support is available at market rates, with no captive processing fees or hidden per-loan charges. You do what you do best, which is originate loans and build relationships, and the model handles the operational machinery around you.

OPERATIONAL COMPLEXITY: RETAIL vs. TRUE BROKER
What you actually manage day-to-day in each model

Operational Area	Retail Bank	True Broker (Edge)
Technology Setup	Company-assigned (overpriced)	Pre-built platform (market rate)
Rate Shopping	One rate sheet, no options	150+ lenders
Compliance	Company handles (charges you)	Company handles (transparent cost)
Processing	Captive processor (per-loan fee)	Your choice of processor (market rate)
Compensation Understanding	Complex splits + hidden deductions	Flat 2.75% - fully transparent
Client Data Ownership	Company owns everything	YOU own your database
Marketing	Company-branded templates	YOUR brand, YOUR content
Daily Experience	Complex, opaque, controlled	Simple, transparent, empowering

Notice something about that chart. In every single row, the true broker model is either equal to or better than the retail model in terms of simplicity. The technology is pre-built. The rate shopping is consolidated into one portal. The compliance is handled. The processing is available at competitive market rates. The only thing that is different is that you can actually see where the money goes, you own your client data, and your brand belongs to you. The retail model is not simpler than the broker model. It is more opaque than the broker model, and opacity is not the same thing as simplicity. It just feels simpler because you have been trained not to ask questions.

The Transparency Revolution

Ray Dalio built the largest hedge fund in the world by making radical transparency the operating philosophy of Bridgewater Associates. He proved that when you force everything into the open, when you eliminate the ability to hide bad decisions behind closed doors, the organization performs better. Not marginally better. Dramatically better. The reason is simple: transparency creates accountability, accountability creates trust, and trust creates performance. Remove any one of those links and the chain breaks.

The mortgage industry has operated with broken chains for decades. Retail banks have built empires on the assumption that loan officers will never see the full revenue picture, will never understand the true cost of the services being deducted from their compensation, and will never question the gap between the value they create and the income they receive. That assumption held for a long time, and it made a lot of people at the top of those organizations very wealthy. But that era is ending, and it is ending for the same reason that every era of institutional opacity eventually ends: someone turned on the lights.

The true broker model is the light switch. When compensation is set at a flat, transparent rate like 2.75%, there is no place to hide extraction. When the loan officer can see every lender's wholesale rate in a single portal, there is no way to bury yield spread profit in a retail markup. When technology costs are purchased at market rates from competing vendors, there is no opportunity to mark up a $65 LOS license and sell it back to the loan officer for $325. When the loan officer owns their client database, there is no leverage in threatening to keep their contacts if they leave. Transparency does not just change the economics of the model. It dismantles the entire system of control that retail banks have used for decades to keep loan officers producing at full capacity while earning a fraction of their value.

THE TRANSPARENCY TEST

Can your current company answer these questions with a straight face?

Transparency Question	Retail Bank	True Broker (Edge)
What is the total revenue on each loan I close?	"That is proprietary"	Visible in the pricing portal
What percentage of revenue do I keep?	"Your comp plan is competitive"	2.75% - $995 company Fee
What does my technology actually cost?	"It is included in your package"	Market rate, you see every invoice
How many people are paid from my loans?	"We are all part of the team"	You, your processor. That is it.
Who owns my client database?	"Company policy protects data"	YOU own it. Always.
What happens to my book if I leave?	"Refer to your employment agreement"	It goes with you. It is yours.
Can I see the wholesale rate before markup?	"You see the retail rate sheet"	You ARE the wholesale channel

Look at the retail column one more time. Every single answer is a deflection. Not one of them is a number. Not one of them is a straight answer. Now look at the broker column. Every answer is direct, specific, and verifiable. That contrast tells you everything you need to know about which model is built on trust and which model is built on information control.

Why Transparency Is the Future of Mortgage

Every major disruption in the history of American business has followed the same pattern. An established industry builds a profitable model based on information asymmetry, which is a fancy way of saying that the company knows things the customer and the workers do not know, and that knowledge gap is where the profit lives. Then technology, regulation, or competition erodes the information gap, and the companies that were built on secrecy either adapt to transparency or they die. It happened in stockbroking when Charles Schwab introduced discount commissions and online trading. It happened in retail when Amazon made price comparison instant and universal. It happened in travel when Expedia and Kayak let consumers see what airlines were actually charging instead of relying on travel agents who earned hidden commissions.

The mortgage industry is in the middle of that exact same disruption right now. The information gap that retail banks have relied on for thirty years is closing, and it is closing fast. Wholesale rate sheets that were once invisible to loan officers are now accessible through broker platforms. Fee structures that were once buried in fifty-page employment agreements are now being documented and shared in books like this one. Compensation models that were once accepted without question are now being compared side by side in online forums, industry podcasts, and recruiting conversations. The loan officers who understand what is happening are moving. The ones who do not are staying, and the gap between those two groups is going to widen every single year.

THE COMPLETE TRUE BROKER ADVANTAGE

Every dimension of the model compared side by side

Dimension	Retail Bank	True Broker	Advantage
CHEAPER			
Borrower Rate	Higher (retail markup)	Lower (wholesale access)	25-75 bps savings or more
LO Tech Costs	$9,600-$19,800/yr	$2,160-$5,700/yr	60-75% less
LO Net Income ($18M vol)	$150K-$165K	$415K-$443K	$250K-$350K MORE
FASTER			
Avg. Close Time	35-45 days	21-30 days	7-15 days faster
Lender Options	1 lender	30-80+ lenders	Total flexibility
EASIER			
Compensation Clarity	Opaque, multi-layered	Flat 2.75%, no surprises	Total transparency
Data Ownership	Company owns clients	YOU own clients	Your business equity
Brand Ownership	Company brand only	YOUR personal brand	Portable reputation

There it is. The complete picture. Cheaper for the borrower. Faster to close. Easier to operate. More profitable for the loan officer. And built entirely on transparency instead of secrecy. If you are reading this and wondering why anyone would stay in retail after seeing these numbers, you are asking the right question. The answer is that most people stay because they have never seen the numbers laid out this clearly, and the people who benefit from the current system have a very strong incentive to make sure they never do.

I want to tell you about a woman named Angela who spent eleven years at a large retail bank in North Carolina. Angela was a top producer. She closed $24 million in volume her best year and averaged $20 million over the last five years of her retail career. Her W-2 showed $195,000 in her best year, and she was proud of that number because it put her in the top twenty percent of earners in her company.

Angela attended a conference where a panel of independent brokers was discussing their business models. She sat in the back row with her arms crossed, convinced she was going to hear a sales pitch wrapped in half-truths. Instead, she heard three brokers share their actual compensation numbers from the previous year. One of them produced the same volume as Angela, twenty million dollars, and his net income after all business expenses was $412,000. Angela went back to her hotel room, sat on the edge of the bed, and called her husband. She told him she had just realized she had left more than two million dollars on the table over the last five years.

Angela transitioned to a true broker model four months later. Her first full year as an independent broker, she produced $22 million in volume, slightly more than her retail average, and her net income was $437,000 (After her expenses). She did not work harder. She did not work longer hours. She did not suddenly become a better loan officer. She was the same Angela with the same skills, the same relationships, and the same work ethic. The only thing that changed was the model around her. The layers of extraction were gone. The hidden fees were gone. The management overrides were gone. The technology markups were gone. And for the first time in her career, she could see exactly where every dollar went.

The part of Angela's story that sticks with me the most is what she told me about her borrowers. She said that in her first year as a broker, she saved her borrowers a combined $412,000 in interest over the life of their loans by placing them with wholesale lenders at rates that were consistently 25 to 50 basis points below what she could have offered them at her old retail bank. Her borrowers were getting better deals, her Realtors were getting faster closings, and she was earning more than double her retail income. Everybody won, except the retail bank that had been taking the lion's share of the value for eleven years.

Angela told me something that I think summarizes this entire chapter better than anything I could write on my own. She said, "Michael, I did not become a broker. I became honest. For the first time in my career, I could look a borrower in the eye and know that I was giving them the best rate available in the market, not just the best rate my company allowed me to show them. That changed everything for me. Not just financially. It changed how I felt about my work."

You have seen the theft. You have asked the questions. You have embraced the CEO mindset. You have seen the true broker advantage. Now it is time to make the move. Chapter 10 gives you the step-by-step playbook for transitioning from retail to independence, and it is simpler than you think.

Chapter 10:
MAKING THE MOVE

CHAPTER 10
Making the Move

"We can choose courage or we can choose comfort, but we cannot have both. Not at the same time."

Brene Brown, Daring Greatly

There is a moment that comes for every retail loan officer who reads a book like this one. It is the moment between knowing and doing. You have read the numbers. You have seen the twelve ways extraction works. You have asked the seven questions, or at least imagined asking them, and you already know what the answers would be. You have done the math on the CEO Loan Officer model. You have seen what the true broker advantage looks like on paper. You know, with a clarity that you did not have before you picked up this book, that you are leaving hundreds of thousands of dollars on the table every single year. And now you are sitting with that knowledge, and it is sitting heavy, because knowledge without action is just a more informed version of being stuck.

Brene Brown has spent her career studying what happens in the space between knowing what you should do and actually doing it. Her research on courage and vulnerability has reached millions of people through her books, her TED talks, and her Netflix specials, and the core finding is always the same: the thing standing between you and the life you want is not information. It is the willingness to be uncomfortable long enough to walk through the door. You can choose courage or you can choose comfort, but you cannot have both. That line is not just a motivational quote for a coffee mug. It is the precise description of the decision you are facing right now.

This chapter is your playbook for walking through the door. I am going to give you the exact steps, the exact timeline, and the exact conversations you need to have in order to transition from retail to independence without burning a single bridge, without violating a single agreement, and without losing a single night of sleep. I have watched hundreds of loan officers make this move, and the ones who do it well all follow the same basic pattern. That pattern is what you are about to learn.

Before You Give Notice: The Quiet Preparation

The transition from retail to independent broker does not start the day you hand in your resignation. It starts weeks or even months before that, in the quiet hours when you are gathering information, building your plan, and laying the groundwork for a clean departure. The goal of this phase is simple: get your house in order so that when the day comes to walk through the door, you are walking into something, not just walking away from something. People who leave retail in a panic, fueled by emotion and frustration, tend to make mistakes. People who leave with a plan tend to thrive.

Step One: Consult an Employment Attorney. Before you do anything else, take your employment agreement, your non-compete clause, your non-solicitation agreement, and any other paperwork you signed when you joined the company, and put all of it in front of a licensed employment attorney in your state. Do not ask your cousin who practices family law. Do not ask your buddy who watches legal dramas. Find an attorney who specializes in employment law, specifically non-competes and non-solicitation agreements, and pay them for an hour of their time. This is the single most important investment you will make in your transition, and it typically costs between $250 and $500. The attorney will tell you exactly what your agreements say, what is enforceable in your state, what is likely unenforceable, and what specific actions you need to take or avoid during your transition to stay on the right side of the law. Many loan officers discover that their non-competes are far less restrictive than they feared, and some discover that their agreements are effectively unenforceable under current state law. But you need to know, not guess, and an attorney is the only person qualified to give you that answer.

Step Two: Secure Your Personal Contacts. Your personal relationships, the ones you built over years of lunches, phone calls, open houses, and late-night emails, are your most valuable business asset. Before you give notice, make sure you have personal contact information for every referral partner, every Realtor, every financial planner, every attorney, and every past client who is part of your professional network, stored in a place that you own and control. This means your personal phone, your personal email contacts, or a personal spreadsheet saved on your personal computer. Do not take anything that belongs to the company. Do not download the company CRM database. Do not export company records. You are simply ensuring that you have your own personal contact information for the people you have personal relationships with. There is a legal and ethical difference between your personal contacts and the company's proprietary database, and your employment attorney will help you understand exactly where that line falls in your state.

Step Three: Choose Your Landing Spot. Research the broker platform or company you want to join before you leave, not after. Talk to loan officers who are already working there. Ask them about the technology, the compensation structure, the compliance support, the processing options, and the culture. If you are considering Edge Home Finance, call us and ask every hard question you can think of. Ask about the 2.75% compensation model. Ask about the wholesale lender relationships. Ask about what happens if you need help with a complicated loan scenario. Ask about what the onboarding process looks like. The more questions you ask before you leave, the more confident you will feel when you do. You should know exactly where you are going, exactly what it costs, and exactly what your first thirty days will look like before you give notice at your current company.

Step Four: Build a Financial Runway. Most loan officers have loans in their pipeline that will close after they leave, and depending on their employment agreement, they may or may not receive commission on those loans. Your employment attorney can advise you on this. Regardless, it is smart to have sixty to ninety days of living expenses saved before you make the transition. This is not because the broker model takes a long time to generate income. Most loan officers who transition with an active pipeline begin closing loans within thirty to forty-five days of moving their license. The financial runway is for your peace of mind. It is the buffer that allows you to make clear-headed decisions during the transition instead of panicking about cash flow. If you and your spouse are both loan officers, stagger your transitions so that one of you has income flowing while the other is getting set up.

PRE-DEPARTURE CHECKLIST

Complete these steps before you give notice

	Action Item	Timeline	Estimated Cost
1	Consult employment attorney	4-8 weeks before	$250 - $500
2	Secure personal contacts in personal device	4-6 weeks before	$0
3	Research and call Michael about Edge Home Finance	3-6 weeks before	$0 (research phase)
4	Build 60-90 day financial runway	2-8 weeks before	Varies by household
5	Complete new company onboarding paperwork	1-2 weeks before	Licensing transfer fees
6	Prepare resignation letter (professional, brief)	1 week before	$0
7	Give notice and begin transition	Day One	Freedom: priceless

The Resignation Conversation: How to Leave With Dignity

When the day comes to give notice, keep it professional, keep it brief, and keep it kind. You are not leaving because your manager is a bad person. You are not leaving because the company did something evil. You are leaving because you have decided to pursue a business model that better serves your financial goals and your clients. That is a business decision, and it deserves to be communicated like one.

Request a private meeting with your direct manager. Sit down, look them in the eye, and tell them that you have made the decision to transition to an independent broker model. Thank them sincerely for the opportunities the company has given you. Tell them that you respect the organization and the people you have worked with, and that you want to make the transition as smooth as possible. Hand them a written resignation letter that is no more than three or four sentences long. The letter should state that you are resigning your position, provide your last day of employment, and express gratitude for the experience. That is all it needs to say. It does not need to explain your reasons, detail your future plans, or reference anything you have learned from this book.

Do not get drawn into a debate about your decision. Your manager may ask why. Your manager may offer a counter. Your manager may tell you that brokers fail, that the market is tough for independents, or that you are making a mistake. They may appeal to loyalty, to the team, or to the relationships you have built in the office. All of those responses are normal, and most of them are sincere. Your manager has every right to feel disappointed and to try to keep a top producer. But you have already made your decision, and re-opening the analysis in a meeting that runs on emotion rather than data is not going to serve you. The appropriate response to every counter-argument is something like this: "I really appreciate that, and I have thought about this for a long time. My mind is made up, but I want you to know that I respect you and I am grateful for everything this company has done for me."

There are three things you should never do in a resignation conversation, no matter how tempted you are. First, do not criticize the company's compensation model. Even if you know exactly how much you have been overpaying for technology, how much the management overrides have cost you, and how much the rate spread extraction has taken from your borrowers, this is not the time to deliver that information. You are leaving, not litigating. Second, do not recruit your colleagues on the way out. Telling other loan officers at the company about the broker model, sharing your compensation numbers, or

138

handing out copies of this book in the break room on your last day is a violation of trust, and in some cases it may violate your employment agreement. If other loan officers come to you later and ask about your experience, that is their choice, but you should never be the one initiating that conversation while you are still employed or recently departed. Third, do not take anything that belongs to the company. Return your laptop, your keys, your badges, and any company-owned materials. Leave your company email account untouched. Walk out clean.

Your First 90 Days: The Transition Playbook

The first ninety days after you transition from retail to the true broker model are the most important days of your new business life. They set the tone for everything that follows. The good news is that you are not starting from scratch. You are the same loan officer with the same skills, the same relationships, and the same reputation. You are not building a business from nothing. You are simply moving that business into a structure that pays you what you are worth. Here is how the ninety days typically unfold.

Days 1 Through 14: Setting Up Shop

Your first two weeks are about infrastructure. Your license transfer is already in process, because you initiated that paperwork before you gave notice. Your new company's onboarding team walks you through the technology setup, which in most modern broker platforms takes two to three days, not two to three weeks. You are learning the pricing portal, which aggregates rates from dozens of wholesale lenders into a single interface. You are setting up your CRM, which you now own and control. You are ordering business cards and setting up your new email signature. You are updating your personal website and social media profiles to reflect your new company. And you are making a list of every Realtor, financial planner, attorney, and past client you intend to contact during weeks two and three.

During this same two-week period, you are also closing any loans that were in your pipeline before you left. Depending on your employment agreement and the arrangement you made with your former employer, some of those loans may close under your old company and some may transfer with you. Your employment attorney already clarified this before you gave notice, so there are no surprises. Either way, you have income coming in within your first thirty days, because you planned the transition around your pipeline rather than leaving with an empty one.

Days 15 Through 45: Announcing Your Move

This is the phase where you reconnect with your network. You are not cold calling. You are not prospecting strangers. You are reaching out to people who already know you, trust you, and have sent you business before. The message is simple and honest: you have transitioned to an independent broker model that gives you access to more lenders, better rates, and faster closings, and you are excited about being able to serve them even better than before.

The conversations will surprise you. Most Realtors do not care what company name is on your business card. They care about you, your responsiveness, your reliability, and your ability to close on time. When you tell a Realtor that you now have access to thirty or more wholesale lenders instead of one retail rate sheet, and that you can shop pricing and turn times across the entire market on every deal, most of them will be impressed. Some will send you a deal that same week just to test the new model. When that first deal closes faster and at a better rate than what you were offering before, you will have a referral partner for life.

Past clients are even easier. A simple message that says you have moved to a new company and that you are now able to offer access to a wider range of lenders and better pricing is all it takes. Most past clients will respond with congratulations and a mental note that you are the person to call the next time they need a mortgage. Some will have a refinance they have been putting off, and your call will be the push they needed. Others will have a friend or family member who is buying a home, and your name will be the first one they mention.

Days 46 Through 90: Building Momentum

By day forty-six, you should be closing loans. Your pipeline is building from referral partner conversations and past client reconnections. You are getting comfortable with the pricing portal and learning which wholesale lenders have the best turn times on different product types. You are discovering that the compliance support from your new company is handling the regulatory details that used to give you headaches at the retail bank. You are seeing your commission statements for the first time, and the numbers are different. Not a little different. Dramatically different. The same loan that earned you $3,750 in retail is now earning you $10,312 at 2.75% on a $375,000 loan. You are doing the same work, serving the same people, and the financial result has changed by a factor of nearly three.

This is also the phase where your confidence solidifies. The fear that kept you in retail, the worry that you could not do this on your own, the anxiety about leaving the perceived safety of a big company, all of it begins to dissolve as you see the real numbers on your real commission statements. You start to understand at a gut level what you already knew intellectually: you were always running a business. You were just paying someone else for the privilege of not calling it one.

YOUR 90-DAY TRANSITION TIMELINE

What to expect and when to expect it

Phase	Key Activities	Expected Results
Days 1-14	License transfer, technology setup, CRM configuration, branding updates, pipeline transition planning	Fully operational platform, first loans submitting to wholesale lenders, income from transitional pipeline
Days 15-45	Realtor reconnection calls, past client outreach, referral partner announcements, first new applications	Pipeline rebuilding, first new closings, Realtor test deals, referral flow resuming
Days 46-90	Steady origination volume, wholesale lender optimization, marketing system launch, brand building	Volume approaching or matching pre-transition levels, commission statements reflecting 2-3x retail income
Day 91+	Full production mode, relationship deepening, volume growth from improved Realtor confidence	Exceeding pre-transition volume as better pricing and faster closings generate more referrals

The Phone Call From Your Old Manager

It is going to come. Somewhere between day three and day thirty, your phone is going to ring, and it is going to be someone from your old company. It might be your direct manager. It might be the regional VP. It might be someone from HR or recruiting. And the conversation is going to follow one of three scripts, all of which I want you to be prepared for, because being prepared is the difference between handling it with grace and getting pulled back into a decision you have already made.

Script One: The Guilt Trip. This is the most common version. Your old manager calls to tell you how disappointed they are. They thought you were loyal. They gave you opportunities. They supported you during slow months. They considered you part of the family. The subtext is that you have betrayed them, and the goal is to make you feel guilty enough to second-guess your decision. The appropriate response is kind but firm. You can say something like: "I appreciate everything you and the team did for me, and I meant it when I said I was grateful. This was a business decision that I needed to make for my family, and I hope you can understand that. I wish you and the team nothing but the best." Then change the subject or end the call. Do not apologize for making a financial decision that benefits your family. You do not owe anyone an apology for choosing to keep the money you earn.

Script Two: The Counter-Offer. This version comes with a carrot. Your old manager or a senior leader calls to offer you a better deal if you come back. Maybe they bump your comp plan by twenty or thirty basis points. Maybe they offer a signing bonus. Maybe they promise to move you to a different branch or give you a better title. The math on counter-offers is always the same, and it always favors the company. A twenty basis point raise on $18 million in volume is $36,000 per year. That sounds significant until you compare it to the $250,000 to $290,000 per year advantage you gain by operating in the true broker model. The counter-offer is designed to buy you back at a fraction of what your independence is worth. The appropriate response is something like: "I am flattered, and I appreciate the gesture. But I have done a lot of research on the economics of the broker model, and I am confident this is the right path for me. I hope we can stay in touch professionally." Do not reveal your new compensation numbers. Do not debate the economics. Just decline with grace and move forward.

Script Three: The Threat. This one is the least common but the most rattling. Someone from the company, usually HR or legal, calls to remind you about your non-compete, your non-solicitation clause, or your obligation to return company property. The tone is formal and sometimes intimidating. The goal is to scare you into freezing, slowing your transition, or avoiding contact with your former clients and referral partners. This is exactly why Step One of the pre-departure checklist was consulting an employment attorney. If you have already done that, you know exactly what your agreement says, what is enforceable, and what is not. The appropriate response is calm, professional, and brief: "I appreciate you reaching out. I have consulted with my attorney and I am confident that I am in full compliance with my agreements. If the company has specific concerns, please have your legal team communicate them to my attorney." Then provide your attorney's contact information and end the call. Do not engage in a legal debate. Do not let fear change your behavior. Let the lawyers talk to the lawyers, and go back to building your business.

THE PHONE CALL RESPONSE GUIDE

Know the script before the phone rings

Script Type	What They Say	What You Say
The Guilt Trip	"We are disappointed. We gave you opportunities. We thought you were part of the family."	"I am grateful for everything, and I meant that. This was a business decision for my family. I wish you and the team nothing but the best."
The Counter-Offer	"What if we raise your comp by 20-30 bps? We can offer a signing bonus to stay."	"I am flattered and I appreciate it. I have done extensive research on the broker model and I am confident this is the right path. I hope we can stay in touch."
The Threat	"We want to remind you of your non-compete and non-solicitation obligations."	"I have consulted with my attorney and I am in full compliance. If the company has specific concerns, please have your legal team contact my attorney directly."

Golden Rule: In every version of this phone call, your tone is warm, grateful, and final. You are not debating. You are not defending. You are informing. The decision has been made, and you are already building something new.

The Bridges You Keep

I called this chapter "breaking free without burning bridges," and I want to spend a moment on why the bridges matter. The mortgage industry is a small world. The branch manager you leave today might be the regional VP at a wholesale lender you want to submit loans to next year. The loan officer who sat in the cubicle next to you might transition to the broker model six months from now and become your closest ally. The compliance officer who reviewed your files at the retail bank might end up at the same wholesale lender you use most frequently. The relationships you build in this industry outlast any single company, and the way you leave a company says as much about your character as the way you operate within one.

I have seen loan officers leave retail banks in every way imaginable. I have seen people storm out of the building after a shouting match with their manager. I have seen people send company-wide emails detailing every grievance they accumulated over ten years. I have seen people recruit half the sales floor on their way out the door. And without exception, every single one of those people regretted the way they left. Not because they were wrong about the economics. They were right about the economics. They regretted it because the way they left defined how people remembered them, and in an industry built on trust and reputation, how people remember you is worth more than any single commission check.

Leave well. Leave with gratitude. Leave with your head high and your handshake firm. Thank the people who helped you, even if the company's compensation model did not serve you. Wish them success, and mean it. Then go build something extraordinary, and let the results speak louder than any exit speech ever could.

The Fear Inventory: What Is Actually Stopping You

Before I close this chapter, I want to name the fears directly, because I have learned that fears lose most of their power the moment you drag them out of the shadows and put them on paper. I have talked to hundreds of loan officers who were considering the transition, and the same fears come up in nearly every conversation. Here they are, along with what the data actually shows.

"What if I lose my Realtors?" You will not lose them. Your Realtors work with you because of you, not because of the logo on your business card. In our experience, eighty to ninety percent of an established loan officer's referral relationships follow them within the first sixty days. The ones who do not follow immediately almost always come back within six months once they see the results you are producing at better rates with faster closings.

"What if I cannot figure out the technology?" You figured out the technology at your last company, and the technology in the broker model is typically simpler, not more complex. Modern broker platforms are designed for individual loan officers, not for enterprise IT departments. If you can use a smartphone and a laptop, you can run the technology stack. And your new company's support team will walk you through every step of the setup.

"What if my non-compete prevents me from working?" This is the fear that keeps more loan officers trapped than any other, and it is almost always overblown. Non-competes in the mortgage industry are notoriously difficult to enforce, particularly for commission-only employees. Many states have passed legislation limiting or prohibiting non-compete enforcement for workers below certain income thresholds or in certain industries. Your employment attorney will tell you exactly what your risk exposure is, and in the vast majority of cases, the answer is far less than you imagined.

"What if I make less money?" You will not make less money. Every set of numbers in this book, from the twelve ways extraction to the CEO P&L to the true broker advantage, points to the same conclusion: loan officers who transition from retail to the true broker model earn significantly more on the same production volume. Not a little more. A lot more. The only scenario in which you make less money is if you stop working, and you are not going to stop working because you did not stop working when you were earning a fraction of your value. You are certainly not going to stop when you can see the full economic result of every loan you close.

"What will people think?" Some people at your old company will think you made a mistake. Some will think you are brave. Some will be jealous. Some will be inspired. And honestly, what they think does not matter nearly as much as what your family thinks when they see the financial trajectory of your new career. Your spouse's opinion matters. Your children's future matters. The opinions of people in an office you no longer work in will fade from your mind within thirty days and from theirs within sixty.

I want to close this chapter with a story about a loan officer named Jim who worked for a mid-size retail bank in Birmingham, Alabama. Jim was forty-three years old, married with three kids, and had been in retail for fourteen years. He produced $16 million in volume and earned $148,000 per year. He read an early version of this book and did the math. He knew he was leaving money on the table. He knew the broker model was better. But he sat on that knowledge for five months, because the fear of change was heavier than the math.

What finally pushed Jim to act was not a spreadsheet. It was a Saturday morning. His oldest daughter, who was sixteen at the time, told him she wanted to visit colleges that summer. Jim looked at his savings account and felt the familiar knot in his stomach that comes when you know the money is not where it should be. Not because he was bad with money. Because the money was never there to be good with. Fourteen years of extraction had left him with a fraction of what he should have accumulated. He told me later that in that moment, sitting at the kitchen table with his daughter's college brochures spread out in front of him, he decided that he was done letting someone else's business model determine his family's financial future.

Jim followed every step in this chapter. He consulted an attorney. He secured his contacts. He researched three broker platforms and chose the one that aligned with his values. He built a sixty-day financial runway. He gave notice on a Monday morning, shook his manager's hand, and walked out with his head high. His manager called three days later with the guilt trip script, and Jim responded exactly the way I described above. He was kind. He was firm. He was final.

Jim's first full year as an independent broker, he produced $17.5 million in volume, slightly above his retail average, and his net income after all business expenses was $389,000. His daughter is now a sophomore at the University of Alabama, and Jim told me that the tuition check he wrote for her freshman year was the proudest check he has ever written. Not because of the amount, but because for the first time in his career, the money was there. It was there because he decided to keep the cash instead of letting someone else keep it for him.

That is the choice in front of you. The same choice that was in front of Angela, Derek and Karen from Nashville, Lisa from Memphis, Todd from Phoenix, and every other loan officer whose story is woven through these pages. They all faced the same fears you are facing right now. They all had the same doubts. And they all decided that courage was more important than comfort. Every single one of them will tell you the same thing: the only regret is that they did not do it sooner.

You have the playbook. You have the timeline. You have the scripts. Now it is time to hear the invitation. Chapter 11 is personal. It is my story, it is our model, and it is your open door.

Chapter 11:
YOUR INVITATION

CHAPTER 11

Your Invitation

"It is in your moments of decision that your destiny is shaped."

Tony Robbins, Awaken the Giant Within

I wrote this book sitting at a desk in my home office at five in the morning, before my twelve kids woke up and the house turned into the beautiful chaos that has defined every morning of my life for the past two decades. I wrote it with a cup of coffee that got cold three times before I remembered to drink it. I wrote it with the door cracked open so I could hear if one of the little ones needed anything, because that is the deal I made with myself a long time ago. Family first. Always family first. And if you have read this far, I believe with everything in me that you made the same deal with yourself, whether you said it out loud or not. You are in this industry because you are trying to build something for the people who depend on you. You are closing loans at nine o'clock at night and returning calls at six in the morning because there are people at your kitchen table who are counting on you to provide, to protect, and to build a future that is better than the present.

That is why this chapter is not a sales pitch. It is an invitation. There is a difference, and the difference matters. A sales pitch is designed to convince you to do something that benefits the person making the pitch. An invitation is designed to open a door and let you walk through it on your own terms, at your own pace, because the person holding the door open believes that what is on the other side is genuinely better for you and your family. I am holding the door open. I have been holding it open for years, and I plan to hold it open for as long as I am in this industry. What you do next is entirely up to you.

How I Got Here

Before I became the person writing this book, I was the person this book was written for. I was a retail loan officer, sitting in a cubicle that someone else owned, using a phone system that someone else paid for, logging into a CRM that someone else controlled, and closing loans that generated enormous revenue for a company that gave me back a small fraction of what I created. I was good at my job. I worked harder than most people around me. I built referral relationships with Realtors and financial planners who trusted me because I cared about their clients the same way I cared about my own family. And every two weeks, I looked at my paycheck and felt a quiet uneasiness that I could not quite name.

That uneasiness did not have a name until I started asking questions. The same questions I shared with you in Chapter 7. When I asked my manager what the total revenue was on the loans I originated, the conversation shifted. When I asked for a breakdown of every fee deducted from my commission, the answers got vague. When I asked who else was being compensated from the loans I closed, the room got uncomfortable. And when I asked the final question, the one about what I would lose by going independent that I could not replace for less money on the open market, my manager paused, looked at me with an expression that was equal parts respect and resignation, and said something I will never forget. He said, "Michael, if you can figure out how to do this on your own, you probably should."

That was the most honest thing anyone in a retail bank has ever said to me, and I have carried it with me every day since. He was not trying to get rid of me. He was telling me the truth, because in that moment, he respected me too much to keep lying. He knew the economics. He knew what I was worth. And he knew that the company's model was designed to capture the majority of my value and redistribute it to a management structure that existed primarily to manage the redistribution. I shook his hand, and three months later, I moved my license.

The first year was not perfect. Nothing worth doing ever is. I learned new systems. I navigated wholesale lender relationships for the first time. I made mistakes with pricing that cost me a few deals. I spent more money on technology than I needed to because I had not yet figured out which tools were worth paying for and which ones were overpriced. But even with all of those growing pains, my income in my first full year as an independent broker was more than double what I had earned in my best year in retail. Not because I worked harder. Because the math changed. The same loans, the same relationships, the same sixty-hour weeks produced a completely different financial result, because the extraction was gone.

That experience is what led me to build Edge Home Finance. I did not build it because I wanted to run a mortgage company. I built it because I realized that the model I had discovered, the true broker model with total transparency, needed to be available to every loan officer who was ready to see the truth and act on it. I built it because I kept meeting loan officers at conferences and industry events who were exactly where I had been: talented, hardworking, dedicated to their clients, and quietly being robbed of the financial future they deserved. I built it because I am a father of twelve, and I believe that every person who works hard enough to build a business deserves to be paid like a business owner, not like a tenant farming someone else's land.

What Edge Home Finance Actually Is

Edge Home Finance is a true broker model built on one principle that governs every decision we make: total transparency. That is not a tagline. It is the operational architecture of the company. Every dollar that flows through a transaction is visible to the loan officer who originated it. Every fee is explained. Every cost is documented. Every compensation calculation is a single, clean number that you can verify on your own in thirty seconds. There are no hidden revenue streams. There are no back-end profits that the company earns on your loans without your knowledge. There are no management overrides, because we do not have a management pyramid. There is no yield spread extraction, because you are the one accessing the wholesale market directly.

Compensation at Edge Home Finance is set at 2.75%. That is not a starting point for negotiation. It is not a ceiling that gets adjusted based on volume tiers or production benchmarks. It is the number. On a $375,000 loan, your compensation is $10,312. On a $500,000 loan, your compensation is $13,750. On

$18 million in annual volume, your gross compensation is $495,000. From that gross number, you pay for your own technology, marketing, and processing at market rates, which we documented in Chapter 8 as ranging from $51,900 to $79,500 per year for a fully equipped independent broker. Your net income on $18 million in volume is $415,500 to $443,100 per year. That is the math, and it does not change based on who you know, how long you have been with the company, or whether your branch manager likes you. It changes based on one variable and one variable only: how many loans you close.

RUN YOUR NUMBERS

Fill in your actual production and see what your income looks like at Edge Home Finance

Your Production Data	Your Retail Numbers	At Edge (2.75%)
YOUR Annual Funded Volume	$_____	(same volume)
YOUR Current Gross Comp (before deductions)	$_____	Volume x 2.75%
Estimated Hidden Deductions (tech, QC, mktg, overhead)	-$_____	$0
YOUR Net Take-Home Pay	$_____	(see below)
Broker Operating Costs (tech, mktg, processing, compliance)	(hidden in split)	-$52K to -$80K
YOUR TRUE NET INCOME	$_____	$_____
THE GAP (what you are leaving on the table every year)		$_____

Annual Volume	Retail Net	Edge Gross	Edge Net	Annual Gap
$12 Million	$100K-$110K	$330,000	$258K-$278K	$148K-$178K
$18 Million	$150K-$165K	$495,000	$415K-$443K	$250K-$293K
$24 Million	$195K-$215K	$660,000	$580K-$608K	$365K-$413K
$36 Million	$285K-$315K	$990,000	$910K-$938K	$595K-$653K
10-YEAR COST OF WAITING (at $18M)				$2.5M - $2.9M

Take a minute with that chart. Find your production level or the one closest to it, and look at the gap column. That number is not the total revenue the company earns on your loans. It is the difference between what you are actually taking home in retail and what you would take home at Edge Home Finance after paying for every single business expense at market rates. It is the net difference. The real difference. The money that is missing from your bank account, your retirement fund, your children's college savings, and your family's financial future every single year that you stay in the current model.

Now multiply that gap by the number of years you plan to keep working. If you are forty years old and you plan to work until you are sixty, that is twenty years. At $18 million in volume, the gap is $250,000 to $293,000 per year. Over twenty years, that is $5 million to $5.86 million. That is not a rounding error. That is not a marginal improvement. That is a generational amount of wealth, the kind of money that changes what college your kids attend, what neighborhood your family lives in, what your retirement looks like, and what you leave behind when you are gone.

What I Promise You

I am not going to promise you that the transition will be effortless, because it will not be. Chapter 10 gave you the playbook, and the playbook works, but there will still be moments in the first ninety days when you feel uncertain. There will be a Tuesday afternoon when a wholesale lender's portal does something you do not expect, and you will have to figure it out. There will be a conversation with a Realtor who wants to know why you left your old company, and you will have to navigate that conversation with grace. There will be a night when you lie in bed and wonder if you did the right thing, and then you will wake up, check your commission statement, and remember exactly why you did.

What I will promise you is this. I promise you total transparency. You will never look at your commission statement at Edge Home Finance and wonder where the money went. You will never discover a fee that was not explained to you before you agreed to it. You will never find out that someone in a management layer you did not know existed was being paid from the revenue you generated. The 2.75% is the 2.75%. There are no asterisks, no footnotes, and no fine print that changes the deal after you arrive.

I promise you ownership. Your client database belongs to you. Your referral relationships belong to you. Your brand belongs to you. If you decide at any point that Edge Home Finance is not the right fit, you take everything you built with you. We do not hold your clients hostage. We do not lock your data behind a proprietary system. We do not enforce non-competes that prevent you from earning a living. You are not a tenant. You are an owner, and owners have the right to leave whenever they choose, with everything that belongs to them.

I promise you support without extraction. You will have access to a team that answers your questions, helps you navigate wholesale lender relationships, supports your compliance requirements, and provides the technology and infrastructure you need to run your business. And that support will never come with a hidden price tag that shows up as an unexplained deduction on your compensation statement. The cost of every service we provide is documented, visible, and competitive with the open market.

And I promise you this, which matters more to me than anything else on this page: I promise you that I will never stop fighting for the loan officers who are still sitting in retail cubicles, still wondering why the math does not add up, still working sixty-hour weeks and feeling like the paycheck does not match the effort. This book is part of that fight. Edge Home Finance is part of that fight. And every loan officer who reads this book, runs the numbers, and makes the move becomes part of that fight too.

The Decision That Shapes Your Destiny

Tony Robbins has spent forty years studying what separates the people who transform their lives from the people who know they should but never do. His conclusion, distilled across millions of people and decades of research, is that transformation does not happen gradually. It happens in a moment. A single moment of decision where you stop negotiating with yourself and start acting on what you already know to be true. Every person who has ever changed their life dramatically, in any arena, for any reason, can point to a specific moment when they decided. Not when they thought about it. Not when they considered it. Not when they gathered more information. When they decided.

You have the information. You have had it since Chapter 2, when we showed you the $26 billion extraction happening across the industry. You have had it since Chapter 3, when David from Charlotte realized that his retail bank had taken $1.7 million from him over eleven years. You have had it since Chapter 7, when the seven questions gave you a framework for proving the extraction at your own company. You have had it since Chapter 8, when the

CEO Loan Officer model showed you that you are already running a business and just not getting paid like it. You have had it since Chapter 9, when the true broker advantage proved that the alternative is cheaper, faster, and easier. And you have had it since Chapter 10, when the transition playbook showed you exactly how to make the move.

The only thing left is the decision.

WHAT HAPPENS NEXT

Two paths. One decision. Your family's financial future.

	If You Stay in Retail	If You Make the Move
This Year	Same income. Same deductions. Same questions without answers.	90-day transition. Income doubles by end of first full year.
In 3 Years	$450K-$495K earned. $750K-$879K left on the table.	$1.25M-$1.33M earned. Business equity building. Brand growing.
In 5 Years	$750K-$825K earned. $1.25M-$1.47M left on the table.	$2.08M-$2.22M earned. College funds growing. Retirement on track.
In 10 Years	$1.5M-$1.65M earned. $2.5M-$2.93M left on the table.	$4.16M-$4.43M earned. Financial independence within reach.
In 20 Years	$3M-$3.3M earned. $5M-$5.86M left on the table forever.	$8.3M-$8.86M earned. Generational wealth created.

Look at the twenty-year row. On the left, you earn $3 million to $3.3 million over a two-decade career and leave $5 million to $5.86 million on the table. On the right, you earn $8.3 million to $8.86 million and leave nothing on the table, because there is no table. There is just you, your clients, and a transparent model that pays you what you are worth. The difference between those two futures is not a new skill, a new market, or a new level of talent. It is a

157

decision. One decision. Made in one moment. And if you are reading this sentence, you are in that moment right now.

A Word From My Kitchen Table to Yours

I started this book by telling you about a vault. A place where the money goes after it is taken from the people who earned it. I told you that I found the combination, and I told you that this book would teach you how to open the door and take back what belongs to you. I hope I have kept that promise.

I am not a Wall Street analyst. I am not a corporate consultant. I am not a thought leader with a fancy title and a corner office. I am a mortgage guy. I am a husband and a father and a man who spent enough years inside the retail system to know exactly how it works and exactly how much it costs the people who make it run. I am also a man who walked away from that system, built something better, and watched hundreds of loan officers do the same thing with results that still make me emotional when I hear their stories. Angela from Charlotte, who doubled her income and started saving her borrowers real money. Derek and Karen from Nashville, who went from $340,000 combined to $867,000. Jim from Birmingham, who wrote his daughter's college tuition check with tears in his eyes because the money was finally there. Lisa from Memphis, who spent eighteen months terrified of a non-compete that her employer never enforced. Tony from Phoenix, who discovered his LOS was marked up 400% and moved his license three months later.

Every one of those stories started the same way yours is starting right now. With a book. With a set of numbers. With a quiet realization that something was not right, followed by the courage to do something about it. They did not have special connections. They did not have MBAs. They did not have trust funds or safety nets or guaranteed outcomes. They had the same thing you have right now: the truth, a plan, and a decision to make.

I want you to take this book home tonight and sit down at your kitchen table with your spouse, your partner, or whoever shares the financial weight of your household with you. I want you to open the Run Your Numbers chart and fill in your actual production. I want you to calculate the gap. And then I want you to sit with that number for as long as you need to, because that number represents the annual cost of staying where you are. Not the cost of risk. Not the cost of change. The cost of standing still.

When you are ready, and I believe you will be, visit keepthecash.com. There you will find the online version of the calculator, a downloadable copy of the Seven Questions Scorecard from Chapter 7, a library of resources for loan officers considering the transition, and a direct line to me and the Edge Home Finance team. We will answer every question you have. We will show you the technology. We will introduce you to loan officers who have made the transition and are willing to share their experience. And we will walk you through the entire onboarding process step by step, because we remember what it feels like to be where you are, and we believe you deserve to know exactly what you are walking into before you take the first step.

I am going to close with something that I do not say lightly, because I have learned in my years as a pastor, a father, and a businessman that words carry weight and should be used with care. You deserve better.

Not because the world owes you something. Not because success should be easy. Not because someone else is responsible for your financial future. You deserve better because you have already done the work. You have already built the relationships. You have already earned the trust of your clients and your referral partners. You have already put in the sixty-hour weeks and the early mornings and the late nights. You have already created the revenue. The only thing you have not done is keep it.

It is time to keep the cash.

READY TO RUN YOUR NUMBERS?

keepthecash.com

Free calculator | Seven Questions Scorecard | Transition resources

Edge Home Finance

Transparent Compensation. Total Ownership. True Independence.

Your clients. Your brand. Your future.

Appendices

The Keep The Cash Toolkit

Everything you need to run your numbers, ask the right questions,
plan your transition, and understand the full scope of extraction.

This toolkit contains four practical resources:

Tool 1: The Compensation Calculator — Run your actual numbers and see the gap

Tool 2: The Seven Questions Worksheet — The questions, how to ask them, and how to score the answers

Tool 3: The Transition Checklist — Your step-by-step playbook for making the move

Tool 4: The 12 Ways Summary — Every extraction method, what it costs, and where to find it in the book

Download interactive versions of all four tools at
keepthecash.com

The Compensation Calculator

This calculator is designed to show you the actual difference between your current retail compensation and what you would earn in a true broker model at 2.75% transparent compensation. Fill in your numbers in the spaces provided. If you are unsure of certain figures, use the estimates provided in the guidance column. For a dynamic, auto-calculating version of this tool, visit keepthecash.com.

SECTION A: YOUR CURRENT RETAIL INCOME

Start with what you know about your current compensation

Line Item	Your Number	Guidance
A1. Your annual funded volume	$_____	Total loans funded this year
A2. Your comp rate (in basis points)	_____ bps	Typically 80-125 bps
A3. Your gross comp before deductions (A1 x A2)	$_____	Volume x bps rate
A4. Technology deductions (LOS, CRM, pricing)	-$_____	$9,600-$19,800/yr typical
A5. Compliance/QC/Legal deductions	-$_____	$9,600-$24,600/yr typical
A6. Marketing/lead program deductions	-$_____	$4,200-$13,200/yr typical
A7. Per-loan fees (processing, doc, admin)	-$_____	$200-$600/loan typical
A8. Other deductions (E&O, desk fees, etc.)	-$_____	Varies by company

A9. YOUR NET RETAIL INCOME (A3 minus A4 through A8)	$_____	This is your real take-home

SECTION B: YOUR INCOME AT EDGE HOME FINANCE (2.75%)

Same production volume, transparent compensation model

Line Item	Your Number	Guidance
B1. Your annual funded volume (same as A1)	$_____	Same volume you do now
B2. Your gross comp at 2.75% (B1 x 0.0275)	$_____	Volume x 2.75%
B3. Technology (LOS, CRM, pricing engine)	-$_____	$2,160-$5,700/yr market rate
B4. Marketing (YOUR brand, YOUR budget)	-$_____	$3,600-$6,000/yr you control
B5. Processing ($500-$750/loan)	-$_____	$24,000-$36,000/yr (48 loans)
B6. Compliance, licensing, E&O insurance	-$_____	$4,800-$6,000/yr typical
B7. Office overhead (if applicable)	-$_____	$0-$12,000/yr (home to office)
B8. Health insurance (if not otherwise covered)	-$_____	$8,400-$18,000/yr family plan
B9. YOUR NET BROKER INCOME (B2 minus B3 through B8)	$_____	This is your real take-home

SECTION C: THE GAP

The annual cost of staying in retail

Calculation	Your Number
C1. Annual Gap (B9 minus A9)	$_____ per year
C2. 5-Year Gap (C1 x 5)	$_____ over 5 years
C3. 10-Year Gap (C1 x 10)	$_____ over 10 years
C4. 20-Year Gap (C1 x 20)	$_____ over 20 years

That C4 number is the total cost of staying in your current model for the remainder of your career. It is not hypothetical. It is the mathematical result of the difference between what you earn and what you could earn, multiplied by time. Visit **keepthecash.com** for the auto-calculating version that does the math instantly.

The Seven Questions Worksheet

These are the seven questions from Chapter 7 that expose the economics of your current compensation model. Print this worksheet, schedule a meeting with your manager, and ask each question directly. Record the response and score it using the color key below. A printable scorecard is also available at keepthecash.com.

GREEN: Clear, specific, numeric answer	YELLOW: Vague, deflecting, partial answer	RED: Refused, hostile, or obviously false

Q1   "What is the total revenue generated on my average loan, from all sources, before any splits or deductions?"

Why it matters: This reveals the full economic value of each loan you close. Typical total revenue ranges from $10,200 to $15,750 per loan on a $375,000 mortgage. If the answer is vague, the company is hiding the number.

Response: _____

Score: Circle one: GREEN   YELLOW   RED

Q2   "Can I see a complete breakdown of every fee and deduction on my commission statement, with an explanation of what each one pays for?"

Why it matters: This exposes hidden deductions. Look for vague labels like "allocation," "overhead," or "technology fee" without specific dollar justification.

Response: _____

Score: Circle one: GREEN   YELLOW   RED

Q3

"What is the total company profit margin on the loans I originate, and what percentage of revenue do I keep versus what the company retains?"

Why it matters: This is the heart of extraction. Typical retail LOs keep 28-35% of total revenue. In the true broker model, LOs keep 70-80%. If the company will not share this number, it is because the number is indefensible.

Response:

_____

Score: Circle one: GREEN   YELLOW   RED

Q4

"If I leave this company, what happens to my client database, my CRM records, and my referral partner contact information?"

Why it matters: This reveals who owns your most valuable asset. If the company keeps your clients when you leave, they own your business equity and you are building their wealth, not yours.

Response:

_____

Score: Circle one: GREEN   YELLOW   RED

Q5

"How many people in the company are compensated, directly or through overrides, from the loans I originate?"

Why it matters: This maps the management pyramid. Typical answer is 7-12 people receiving overrides, bonuses, or allocations from each loan you close. Each one represents a layer of extraction between your production and your paycheck.

Response:

_____

Score: Circle one: GREEN   YELLOW   RED

Q6 "What is the actual cost to the company for the technology, marketing, and compliance services that are deducted from my compensation?"

Why it matters: This exposes 200-400% markups on captive services. The company charges you $200-$400/month for an LOS that costs them $50-$100/month at enterprise volume. Same pattern repeats across CRM, marketing, and compliance.

Response:

_____

Score: Circle one: GREEN   YELLOW   RED

Q7 "If I were to leave and become an independent broker, what specific services would I lose that I could not replace on the open market for less money?"

Why it matters: This is the moment of truth. It forces the company to justify the extraction economically. If they cannot name a single service that is unavailable or cheaper through them, the value proposition of employment collapses.

Response:

_____

Score: Circle one: GREEN   YELLOW   RED

YOUR SCORECARD RESULTS

5-7 GREEN	Rare. Your company is unusually transparent. Still run the compensation calculator to see if the economics justify staying.
3-4 GREEN, rest YELLOW	Partially transparent. The company is willing to share some information but hides the numbers that matter most. Start doing the math seriously.
3+ RED	Your company is actively hiding its economics from you. This is a strong signal that the extraction is significant. Explore your options.
5+ RED	You are inside an extraction machine. This is not a career question. It is a financial survival question. Read Chapter 10 tonight.

The Transition Checklist

This checklist walks you through every step of the transition from retail to the true broker model, organized into three phases. Check off each item as you complete it. Refer to Chapter 10 for detailed guidance on every step.

PHASE 1: BEFORE YOU GIVE NOTICE (4-8 Weeks Out)

Action	Target Date
☐ Consult employment attorney about non-compete and non-solicitation agreements	___/___/___
☐ Secure personal contact information for all referral partners and past clients in a personal device	___/___/___
☐ Research and evaluate broker platforms (interview LOs already working there)	___/___/___
☐ Select your broker platform and begin onboarding paperwork	___/___/___
☐ Build 60-90 day financial runway (living expenses in savings)	___/___/___
☐ Initiate license transfer with new company	___/___/___
☐ Prepare brief, professional resignation letter	___/___/___
☐ Clarify pipeline transition plan with attorney (which loans close where)	___/___/___

PHASE 2: GIVING NOTICE AND FIRST 14 DAYS

Action	Target Date
☐ Give notice in private meeting with direct manager (professional, brief, grateful)	___/___/___
☐ Return all company property (laptop, keys, badges, materials)	___/___/___
☐ Complete new company technology setup (LOS, CRM, pricing portal)	___/___/___
☐ Order new business cards and update email signature	___/___/___
☐ Update personal website and social media profiles	___/___/___
☐ Build outreach list for Realtors, past clients, and referral partners	___/___/___
☐ Prepare responses for The Phone Call (guilt trip, counter-offer, threat scripts)	___/___/___

PHASE 3: DAYS 15-90 AND BEYOND

Action	Target Date
☐ Begin Realtor reconnection calls (personal, not mass email)	___/___/___
☐ Send past client announcements (personal message about your move)	___/___/___
☐ Submit first new loan applications through wholesale portal	___/___/___
☐ Close first loans and review commission statements for accuracy	___/___/___
☐ Optimize wholesale lender selection (best rates, best turn times by product type)	___/___/___
☐ Launch personal marketing system (your brand, your content, your database)	___/___/___
☐ Celebrate: production volume approaching or exceeding pre-transition levels	___/___/___

The 12 Ways They Extract Your Wealth

This is the complete summary of all twelve extraction methods documented throughout the book. Each entry includes the method, the annual cost range, the chapter where it is fully explained, and a one-line description of how it works. Use this as a quick reference guide and as a conversation tool when discussing the economics of retail mortgage banking with colleagues who are considering the transition.

#	Extraction Method	Annual Cost	Ch.	How It Works
1	Rate Spread Theft	$36,000-$97,200	3	Company marks up wholesale rates 25-75 bps and keeps the spread as hidden revenue the LO never sees
2	Basis Point Shell Game	$36,000-$54,000	3	Your comp plan says 100 bps but actual take-home is 60-80 bps after deductions, fees, and split adjustments
3	Management Override Tax	$9,000-$27,000	4	Branch manager earns 5-15 bps override on every loan you close. You fund their income directly.
4	Regional VP Extraction	$5,400-$18,000	4	Regional VP earns 3-10 bps override on your loans plus bonuses tied to your branch production
5	Corporate Overhead Bloat	$10,200-$21,000	4	C-suite, HR, IT, legal, accounting, and facilities all funded by per-loan allocations from your production

6	LOS Technology Scam	$1,200-$3,600	5	Company charges $200-$400/month for LOS license that costs $50-$100/month at enterprise rates
7	CRM Data Con	$1,200-$3,600	5	You pay $100-$300/month for a CRM that stores YOUR clients on THEIR server. When you leave, they keep the data.
8	Quality Control Fees	$3,600-$9,600	5	$75-$200 per loan for QC department that protects the company from regulatory risk, not you
9	Legal Department Extraction	$2,400-$6,000	5	You fund the legal team that writes the non-competes designed to prevent you from leaving
10	Lead Program Scraps	$2,400-$7,200	6	Pay $200-$600/month for leads that convert at 2-5%. Company owns the client from their lead forever.
11	Marketing Mirage	$1,800-$6,000	6	Pay $150-$500/month for generic templates that build the company brand, not yours. Same budget could build YOUR brand.
12	Non-Compete Prison	$162K-$291K/yr	6	Fear of a 12-24 month restriction keeps you trapped. Each extra year of fear costs the full annual gap.

WAYS 1-11: Direct Annual Extraction	$111,600 - $217,200 per year
WAY 12: Annual Opportunity Cost of Staying	$162,000 - $291,000 per year
TOTAL ANNUAL COST (extraction + opportunity)	$273,600 - $508,200 per year
20-YEAR CAREER COST	$5.47M - $10.16M

Download interactive versions of all four tools at
keepthecash.com

You have the tools. You have the truth. Now keep the cash.

WORKS CITED

Brown, Brene. *Daring Greatly: How the Courage to Be Vulnerable Transforms the Way We Live, Love, Parent, and Lead*. New York: Gotham Books, 2012. Print.

Clear, James. *Atomic Habits: An Easy and Proven Way to Build Good Habits and Break Bad Ones*. New York: Avery, 2018. Print.

Cardone, Grant. *The 10X Rule: The Only Difference Between Success and Failure*. Hoboken, NJ: John Wiley & Sons, 2011. Print.

Dalio, Ray. *Principles: Life and Work*. New York: Simon & Schuster, 2017. Print.

Ferriss, Timothy. *The 4-Hour Workweek: Escape 9-5, Live Anywhere, and Join the New Rich*. Expanded and Updated Edition. New York: Harmony Books, 2009. Print.

Godin, Seth. *Linchpin: Are You Indispensable?* New York: Portfolio / Penguin, 2010. Print.

Greene, Robert. *The 48 Laws of Power*. New York: Viking Penguin, 1998. Print.

Housel, Morgan. *The Psychology of Money: Timeless Lessons on Wealth, Greed, and Happiness*. Petersfield, Hampshire: Harriman House, 2020. Print.

Kiyosaki, Robert T., and Sharon L. Lechter. *Rich Dad Poor Dad: What the Rich Teach Their Kids About Money That the Poor and Middle Class Do Not!* Scottsdale, AZ: TechPress, 1997. Print.

Robbins, Tony. *Awaken the Giant Within: How to Take Immediate Control of Your Mental, Emotional, Physical and Financial Destiny!* New York: Simon & Schuster, 1991. Print.

Taleb, Nassim Nicholas. *Skin in the Game: Hidden Asymmetries in Daily Life*. New York: Random House, 2018. Print.

FINAL WORD

Look, I've spent the last 100+ pages showing you how the mortgage industry works, where the money goes, and how to protect yourself. But here's what matters most: you now have a choice. You can walk into the future of your career armed with knowledge, or you can go in blind and hope for the best. Hope is not a strategy, and the industry is counting on you to stay confused.

Do your research. Ask the hard questions. Call me, someone who welcomes transparency instead of hiding behind industry jargon and "proprietary information" excuses. The smoke and mirrors act that the industry teaches only works on people who don't know the tricks. You know them now. Use that knowledge. Edge Home Finance will respect you more for asking tough questions, not less. And if they don't respect you for being informed, they don't deserve you as a loan officer.

I've got twelve kids, and every single one of them would get this advice before they work in the mortgage industry. I'm not going to let them walk into a career and $MILLIONS because some manager saw an easy mark. This book is the same advice I'm giving them, and I'm giving it to you for the same reason: because I have a choice.
1-I can go through life and be a "SUCCESS" and win awards, and be the best. That is all about me.
2-I can go through like and be a "SURVIVOR" and talk about everything I have overcome and how it made me better. That is also about me.
3-I can make the choice to be "SIGNIFICANT". This is about YOU. Can I wake up every single day I find a way to give myself to others.

If you want more straight talk about money, careers, parenting, and navigating life's biggest decisions without getting ripped off, follow me at @DadWith12Kids. I'll keep telling you the truth, even when it makes people uncomfortable. That's what dads do.

Now go keep your cash.